A VISUAL PALETTE

A VISUAL PALETTE

✦

A Philosophy of the Natural Principles of Painting

Kevin Weckbach

iUniverse, Inc.
New York Bloomington Shanghai

A VISUAL PALETTE
A Philosophy of the Natural Principles of Painting

iUniverse books may be ordered through booksellers or by contacting:

iUniverse
1663 Liberty Drive
Bloomington, IN 47403
www.iuniverse.com
1-800-Authors (1-800-288-4677)

ISBN: 978-0-595-52422-8 (pbk)
ISBN: 978-0-595-62476-8 (ebk)

Printed in the United States of America

To My Wife and Daughter,
Natsu and Hana
And, to all who seek truth in life

Contents

ACKNOWLEDGMENTS

Along my path as an artist, I had the great fortune to find a teacher who enlightened me about the philosophical principles of the visual dialogue in painting. In 1993, as a student at the Art Students League of Denver, I met Quang Ho soon after completing my MFA at the Rocky Mountain College of Art and Design. This book shares many of the ideas that Quang Ho routinely taught at the Arts Students League, ideas that opened my eyes, heart and mind to new ways of seeing and engaging in the creative process of painting. With respect and heartfelt thanks to Quang, I am passing on those concepts in this book. In doing so, I aim to articulate what is universally truthful about painting. Just as Quang's journey and the application of these principles were unique to him, so have I made his teachings singularly significant in my own creative journey. I hope you will do the same.

INTRODUCTION

What does it take to reach a higher level of artistic expression in your work? Talent, ambition, a profound understanding of methods and materials—these are all musts. But also needed is the ability to identify great art when you see it and the will to apply its principles in creating your own body of work. There is a certain thirst that drives an artist to gain further knowledge about what makes a "great" painting, and then to apply those criteria to his or her own work. I recall the days when I had no real way to articulate why I thought one painting worked and another failed. Intellectually, I knew there was a rationale by which experts measured what made a "masterpiece," but what that rationale was remained a complete mystery to me. Were those criteria defined by society? Did a given work have to belong to an established school of painting—an "-ism"? Or was the term "masterpiece" ascribed only to those works of artists who had been anointed by some divine deity? I was certain that masterpieces had to possess some higher measure of visual logic, which made them work; otherwise, their value as art would have been purely arbitrary. And if their value was purely arbitrary, then any given painting could be deemed a masterpiece, and any work hanging in a museum could move in and out of favor on a daily basis. Lacking the understanding of what truly made a masterpiece work, I began to distrust the critics and historians. Their judgments seemed arbitrary, and I found myself wondering if the "experts" misunderstood the truth behind painting and claimed them to be masterpieces when in fact they were coming apart at their seams.

If a painting worked, I wanted to know why. I needed a true system of visual logic that could be applied to all paintings in order to determine what constituted an artistic masterpiece. So I began my journey with an open mind and a demand for honesty that was not going to let me settle for half-baked theory or fashionable opinion—I wanted concrete answers.

This book presents the fruits of that journey: a no-nonsense way of looking at and understanding paintings. It will help you to develop the critical capacity to see the value of any work and to frame your own unerring aesthetic judgments. Although this ability is invaluable to collectors and aficionados, it is an absolute must for artists. In order to reach a higher level of artistic expression, a painter must be honest about his or her own work. If he can't determine for himself what is valuable in the canon of masterpieces that make up our artistic tradition, how can he make honest critical judgments about his own work? I have written this book to dispel some of the cant and myth that has taken hold of art criticism, and to replace superstition with a commonsense approach based on universal principles. Although I did not create these principles, through the luck of having had good teachers, I have learned to appreciate them and put them to work in evaluating my own painting. These concepts are based not on my own personal beliefs or prejudices, but on solid visual principles. The job of the book is to explain how "the art of seeing" works in purely visual terms, and how we can translate that knowledge onto canvas as visual poetry.

Although I'm addressing this book to artists, it is intended for anyone who wants to understand painting from a painter's perspective. Whether you have painted for twenty years or have never lifted a brush, this book will deepen your understanding of paintings—how they work and why they matter. Whether you run a gallery or just want the ability to "read" the paintings hanging in a museum or on your living room wall, this book will teach you to how to decide for yourself what is valuable and enduring in the pieces before you.

To begin with, lets do away with the myth that painting cannot be taught, and that only a select few with artistic gifts can understand its principles. Although artistic geniuses are sometimes born, you needn't be a Van Gogh or Rembrandt to build an innate understanding of visual logic. Like any science, the logic of painting exists on a simple cognitive level. Its principles are based on understanding the behavior and interaction of shapes. The laws of painting are defined by the interaction of shape, value and color, principles available to all who will look for themselves. I am simply providing a map that will enable you to understand the logic of these laws by explaining the rationale behind the act of painting.

As we shall see, the act of painting applies an organizing logic to the creative process in a way that renders on canvas a single coherent and compelling statement. It requires the organizing logic of seeing clearly and the act of expressing that vision, in order for the whole plan to work as one visual idea. For a painting to make a powerful visual statement, it must be based on the logic of sound visual principles. To understand these principles, we'll start with the three distinct ways in which we perceive and express our surrounding reality—the first, second and third levels of painting. We'll then examine the particulars of how we break down these levels of perceptions into visual approaches, or "experiences" of light, and the underlying elements of the visual grammar that make up their expression.

This is not a book about techniques, methods or materials; nor does it promote a history of specific artistic styles or movements or "-isms." Neither materials nor history can truly explain what makes a painting work as a successful piece of art. Although that information is readily handy, it won't contribute to an understanding of the visual dialogue that constitutes a painting. Instead, we will look directly at how paintings are constructed (without becoming distracted by all of the "art history" hype surrounding them). We won't attempt to categorize paintings and artists into separate groupings based on style and influence; instead, we will look at them as participants in the same visual act of creation. Since this is an open-minded approach to painting, I urge you to set aside any critical assumptions that may interfere with your understanding of visual logic in its purest form. It may be asking for a lot of trust on my part, but we'll need a leap of faith to overturn old visual habits. It is important to approach this work with a clear mind, and fresh eyes unburdened by old rules. Think of starting this work, as if you were facing a blank canvas.

A Visual Palette examines the reservoir of understanding that artists have gained and applied to the art of painting in the six hundred years they have been actively and self-consciously engaged in the expression of visual reality. With each master painter adding to this understanding and helping it to evolve, it now contains the accumulated knowledge of how we experience and articulate life in purely visual terms. The creative force of this expression has carried us from the early, strange works of Bosch and has propelled us onto the shores of de Kooning's abstract sensibility. And our sails still have wind in them to push us into new territories. It is now a splendid time to be an artist, to build on these lessons of the past and explore new territories.

Cramming six hundred years into a volume as slim as this is a daunting undertaking, but as I've found over twenty years as a working artist, the first rule of painting is, "Don't panic." (It's still one of my favorite reminders when I've feeling pressured in the studio.) There may be a lot that has been unearthed in six-hundred years, but it should not take us that long to explore it. The major developments in painting are easy to spot because they have evolved with a clear compelling logic that is reasonable and sensible, even to an untrained eye. In due time you will grasp the arc of this fascinating story, but it will take patience at first—rushing through will only weaken your understanding. Think of the process like reading a novel: if you skim through it you may know the plot, but you won't have a full understanding of the motivation behind the characters' actions. If you read word-for-word, allowing yourself to be drawn into the reality of the characters, by the time you finish the book you will have a full understanding of a new world and its inhabitants. In a larger sense, this also holds true for the painter's journey: for the artist, it doesn't matter how soon you arrive, but how you get there. Take time to explore this landscape. Respect the process. A humble approach always bears more fruit.

As an artist working within a great visual tradition, you are but a single instrument in a vast orchestra. Your understanding and application of its visual principles uniquely defines you. You may aspire to become an outstanding soloist, but you must still learn to blend with the other instruments. As an artist, the goal of your journey is to find your unique place in this scheme and to realize your expressive potential. As your creative discoveries move you along the path, you will find yourself, in turn, inspiring others. What you give to, and take from, the process belongs at once to you and everyone else. Once you let go of the false sense of separation between yourself and others, and stop comparing, you will progress quickly because there will be nothing to hold you back from the truth.

As a teacher, I constantly try to keep this in mind. When I look at a students' work, I try to get at the underlying visual statement. I then try to gauge my critique to push them to the limit of their ability. If I compared their work to that of other students, or to my own work, I would never see the underlying potential and I wouldn't know how to meaningfully suggest a direction for the work. The artistic path may be lonely at times, but it always seems to provide a helping hand along the way. This is why I teach and the reason I wrote this book—to lend a hand. Having had help, I hope to return the favor. All master painters have made this trek and once stood where you stand now—we are all traveling this same path.

1

THE THREE VIRTUAL LEVELS OF PAINTING

In conveying the expression of visual truth, the art of painting occurs on one of three virtual levels, each of which reflect the artist's depth of perception and expression. The first-level artist is concerned with a literal portrayal of the subject: she records exactly what lies before her. The second-level artist takes greater license in exploring the subject, departing from the objective reality by methodically breaking it down into visual elements. The second-level artist then recombines these elements into a creative expression, which, in turn, may exist independently of the perceived subject. The third-level artist continues this exploration from a more intuitive state of mind, and the resulting work reaches a level of expression that becomes, in itself, an inspired visual event independent of any source or subjective reference. An artist may fluctuate between all three levels, depending on her visual awareness at any given moment. At certain times an artist may perceive the painting on first-level terms, and in the next painting may inhabit the third or second level. However, she will inhabit only one of these three levels in any given painting.

The First Level of Painting: The Literal or Recording Reality

The first-level artist creates a painting from a perception of the world seen in literal terms, and cannot separate the subject from its fundamentally realistic makeup. This artist organizes his painting into a literal rendering of the subject before him. As these subjects may portray religious, mythic, social or political content, their rendering is uniformly literal. Rarely does the first level artist explore the visual elements that comprise the subject; instead, he puts his focus on recreating the subject in its literal context. This literal rendering is more about recapturing a perceived or imagined moment of reality than creating a visual event with its own dynamic reality in the present.

First-level painting always conforms to and defines itself through accepted norms of perception. These works are often judged as rightly or wrongly rendered, depending on the viewer's taste and on how well the paintings conform to the viewer's knowledge and assumptions about the subject. Working in this realm of known visual response, the first-level painter depicts objects, scenes and motifs that can easily be categorized in a way that conforms to the expectations of the viewer and the marketplace. The first-level artist paints for ulterior motives: money, fame, social or political statement, "-ism," or style. None of these categories attempt to depict the fundamental visual reality or creative experience of seeing; instead, they seek to confirm preconceived aesthetic norms. They appeal to the comforts of the conventional, rather than to the exploration of visual truth.

Cracking the Conceptual Shell

Before photography, painting played an important role as a "recording" medium. It operated necessarily on the first-level, providing visual chronicles, portraits, historical tableaus, and recreations of mythical, biblical, dramatic and literary scenes. Painting had a literal function, depicting narrative events. But when the narrative content overwhelmed the visual statement, and painting attempted to supplant drama or history, we generally ended up with bad visual statements of important historical events. Over time, with the advent of printing technology and mass reproduction of the painted image, the iconic function of painting—to create an image of individuals or important fictive and historical events—became even more powerful as an instrument of mass media. The figures depicted became icons within the culture, but so too the styles used to depict these figures and events assumed iconic standing. In the modern era, impressionism, cubism, surrealism, expressionism came to characterize ways of seeing that related ways of depicting visual reality—styles of seeing—that became genre-like in the expectations that they created in the mind's eye of their viewers. The first-level conformation to subject soon embraced a conformation to style. The public began to look for painting to conform not only to familiar subjects, but to a preconceived ways of rendering as well.

Unless they are painters, collectors or students, most viewers of paintings are unconscious of the visual language that paintings speak. Perhaps only ten percent of the public has an interest in art at any given time, but at some point everyone interacts with paintings in one way or another. How most viewers gather their basic understanding of art comes from what they see and hear about it in public spaces, in films, at museums and so on. When asked to think of a masterpiece, just about everyone pictures da Vinci's *Mona Lisa*, though few can explain why it is a masterpiece. While the works of artists such as Manet or Sargent are more unfamiliar to the public—and those of Wyeth or de Kooing, almost unknown—the *Mona Lisa* has become an iconic symbol for the "idea" of a painted masterpiece. The meaning and reason for its appreciation may have disappeared long ago, but today the public reads the *Mona Lisa* as a symbol of what a masterpiece should look like.

One who is trained to look beyond the critical cant surrounding a well-known painting can read the work as a visual statement and see it for what it truly is. In this sense, a painting's visual statement is locked inside like a nut. Critical habits of mind and received opinion act like a shell that keeps us from penetrating the visual reality within. Because the general public understands art on a first-level basis, it reinforces the need for first-level artists to create work that is easily appreciated. Most viewers will identify the subject of a painting or reject it out of hand because the subject cannot be "read" or easily identified. They see the work so superficially that they stop at the subject and cannot identify the visual statement going on beneath the mantle of "masterpiece" or "icon." Because they lack the visual intelligence to penetrate the surface meaning, they lose confidence in their own judgment and give up on the aesthetic experience. Just as a second-level artist is one who can crack through the conceptual shell to get at the heart of the matter inside.

To the novice art student, still unaware of how to look at art, much of his understanding is based on misinformed assumptions. We are all shaped by what we see and hear, but when we are uncertain of what to look for in a painting, we might be inclined to rely on information that is not grounded. A teacher may misinform, and the novice, having no way to test the truth of those assumptions, takes it as fact. Teachers frequently don't know how to read a paintings for themselves, and their teachings are often based on received or wrong-headed, opinion.

It is popular and easy to teach the "-isms"—those mythic schools of aesthetic thought that have come to define much of art criticism today. Although the artists did not intend to create these "-isms," their methodologies have come to define styles of painting and dictate popular understanding of broad areas of artistic endeavor. One could say that a certain painter paints impressionistically, yet the term doesn't necessarily speak to the work's quality. An "-ism" is really just a way to define a certain look for a painting, and nothing more. Individual artistic style defines how an artist translates the subject into shapes, colors, textures and values. It is a unique signature that characterizes an artistic personality, yet it is not necessarily a reliable measure of the paintings aesthetic quality.

Aesthetic beauty is what defines a painting's integrity. It needn't have a pretty look about it. A painting can be ugly or harsh and still hold together aesthetically. For example, there is prettiness to Monet's water lilies compared to Egon Schiele's nudes, yet the works of both artists hold together with a visual clarity that makes them equally beautiful. Neither artist waved a manifesto to proclaim the merits of his particular "-ism"; he just painted the world about him with a clarity and focus that brought to life unique and compelling visual statements in remarkably different styles. It was the cadre of critics fomenting a public clamor that labeled them at a later date.

Style is an arbitrary factor, unique to every artist's personality. To teach style alone is to ground perception on the surface shell of the nut—on the "-ism"—rather than penetrating to the visual reality within. When a teacher speaks of visual integrity and sets aside the "-ism," he begins to speak about what makes a painting work, about the visual play that brings it to life. Painters, in particular, should never choose a style by which they define themselves; instead, they should let the style choose them. An artist may find that she has been painting in a certain style or format because it was taught to her. If so, she should move on. It is a tough habit to overcome, but it can be broken if one grounds one's aesthetic in purely visual principles. Let your painting reflect your natural interpretation of the visual reality. Let go of the "-isms."

An "-ism" provides an easy way to establish an artistic identity, but it is not what fuels the creative process. The list of "-isms" carries on like a skipping record, never resolving what painting is about, or what makes great art. There are literally hundreds, all trying to define themselves and take a piece of the critical pie.

Getting at the Pure Visual Essence

In the broadest stylistic sense, all artists fit somewhere on the spectrum between realism and abstraction, but understanding the visual integrity of a painting—how it works as a piece of art—is based on knowing how to abstract the visual elements from the subject in any given work. Not to be confused with the style of painting made popular in the 40's, 50's and 60's, abstraction as an ordering principle draws away from a conceptual attachment to the subject. It distills the underlying visual essence from the literal subject, as if it existed "on the surface of the eye," as the early 20th century painter and critic Harold Speed said. Once you have reduced the content of a given subject to the bare essentials of its visual elements, you can depict it as an arrangement of shapes. By taking those shapes and assembling them into a composition that the whole painting speaks about, you create a unique and compelling visual statement.

By seeing the subject in purely abstracted terms, you communicate directly with the source of the visual impulse that inspired the work, and can begin to express what the painting is truthfully about. Through the process of engaging the fundamental visual elements, you draw out the visual purity of the subject. In this sense, we are all "abstract" painters. No matter what you paint, or in what style—realism or abstraction—by locating a subject's visual core, you direct your attention to the root source of the painting's interest. You are engaged in distilling the visual truth and in assuming a *bona fide* approach to painting. Even a realistic painting should emphasize design elements that build abstract shapes into a comprehensive visual statement. In this sense, a realist remains true to the visual essentials, not a copyist.

The art of seeing is about rendering the essence of perceived life, not duplication. When you look at a still life with a cup, you instinctively see the cup and, therefore, think, "cup." The natural inclination of a first-level artist is to install that cup into the painting as a cup, emphasizing the feel and function of the subject. The misconception lies in the way that the cup is first stated: if we think and then say to ourselves, "cup," then we are already failing to see it from a painterly perspective. But if we look past the literal designation to see the value and color of the subject—and state those elements to ourselves—we are already getting into the subject's visual anatomy. The downfall of the first-level artist is that he labels the object as a thing, defining it to himself verbally, instead of visually. The art of seeing is based on an abstraction that draws a visual resonance from the subject. It extracts the visual elements and dispels its literal label. A cup transcends its "cupness" and becomes a pattern of shapes, values and color harmonies that make us forget the labels that we stick onto it. If we rely on the label to define it, we are seeing only its symbolic function as a cup. In order to paint a subject honestly, we must remove its literal label and see it in its pure visual essence.

Symbols

Although symbols are perceived as metaphorical in paintings, they still function similarly to literal objects in their impact on the visual statement. Functional symbols surround us in our daily lives, on doors, maps, logos, highways, and so on. Ideographs predated alphabets as a way to communicate, and they still form the basis for Asian languages. We can surmise that cave paintings, which show no apparent consciousness, were used primarily to communicate an event. They weren't intended as visual statements that explored the shapes themselves. There was a normative way of drawing a deer or other object that remained consistent, so that the "reader" would not become confused. The deer painting was a linguistic or discursive element—not a visual exploration. Symbols assembled in a certain order made sense, and their associated sounds evolved into the formal array of letters that composed words—and so language was born.

Language is a learned skill, just as painting is. But in painting, there is no dictionary or grammar book to pick up when we get confused, so it takes a good understanding of how that visual language works. Initially, we look for something familiar to associate to, and so ascribe meaning. One who is unfamiliar with the language of painting will continue to look for identifiable images or icons to give meaning to the work. If she encounters a more abstract work and can't recognize a shape or ascribe meaning to it, the viewing process quickly becomes intimidating. Since there is no dictionary to provide a quick definition of why a shape is the way it is, the viewer may assume the shape is a good one, or she may determine the whole painting to be badly painted because it's visual elements are illegible.

When you approach a painting with a visual vocabulary of shape, you are already reading it with the right mindset. [The meaning of shape is not normative, but relative. Its line or mass always exists in relation to nearby lines or shapes. The true meaning of painting exists in a non-literal realm similar to that of music, where lines of melody and masses of harmony interact without discursive purpose or meaning.] It takes visual awareness to read a painting, yet the more one can read on a visual level the more legible all paintings become. When the visual aspects are read sympathetically, a painting begins to unlock its riches.

First and foremost a painter must construct his work from visual elements, putting them together the way a composer will arrange chords and strings of notes. Like literal or historical content, symbols should never take predominance over the visual statement. They may work in conjunction with visual elements, but psychological or social statement should always take a back seat to visual integrity. If you rely predominantly on imagery to make the painting's statement, you are not working from a visual framework. Only visual integrity supports painterly composition; everything else is secondary.

Subject matter is particular, but visual integrity is universal. A cow may mean food to one person, but convey religious significance for another. To read a painting in visual terms, you must ground your sense of logic in universal aesthetic principles of harmony, contrast, and rhythm—to name a few—that transcend religious, political, sexual and racial concerns. Social conventions and norms change with time, but the aesthetic principles that shape the visual integrity of painting remain a constant.

The Abstract Motive

Needless to say, if you look at an abstract painting expecting to find a concrete depiction of an apple or a figure, you are barking up the wrong tree. Any good painting—realistic or abstract—should hold together abstractly as an orchestration of shape, because it is the rendering of that underlying visual dialogue that ultimately determines the painting's success as a visual statement. Abstract painting removes the literal object as a reference, so the viewer directly confronts the immediacy of pure visual interaction. For better or worse, an uneducated eye will praise a realistic painting because it looks recognizable; but when there is no object to serve as a reference to anchor that appreciation, the callow viewer will not be able to read the artist's visual statement on its own merits.

Since abstract painting portrays the pure interaction of visual elements, the myth has arisen that it is somehow dissociated from life. In fact, abstract painting frequently draws from visual relationships found in everyday objects. Rather than painting from sheer imagination, De Kooning was famous for finding his shapes in household objects in his studio. He protested vehemently against the terms "non-objective" and "action" painting, because he believed that he was always painting from life. A non-objective painter is one who paints shapes instead of recognizable subjects, yet the title might apply to the realist and abstract painter alike, if they both paint for the visual essence and not the object.

A realist is not any greater or lesser an artist than the abstractionist. What makes a realistic painting resemble a real person, place or thing is the completion of shape into recognizable objects. Abstract painting is just as demanding and requires the same superb level of draftsmanship to instill quality into its renderings of shape. In abstract painting your visual acuity and drawing skill must be finely tuned, because you have no objects to reference. You must invent or draw from your environment in order to form the shapes are unique and complete. A good realist knows this and applies it as well, but that level of invention and adaptation is often not apparent in their work because it appears to reference a given subject. Those who cannot appreciate the quality of shape when the literal reference is cut loose from the painting will miss the integral quality of the abstract painting experience. The uninitiated will always need shape to look like something, so that they can have the security of a comparable reference to anchor their perception. But, in fact, it is always the underlying abstraction that structures a painting—realistic or non-objective.

Abstraction is predominantly a way to feature shape in a painting, but it is not a good way to define yourself as a painter. If you seek the underlying interaction of shape, form and color in your work, regardless of whether its content is real objects or pure invention, you will paint abstractly. But if you label yourself an abstractionist, simply because you don't paint recognizable objects, you are reverting back to the first-level seeing. For both the realist and the abstractionist, abstraction is an ordering principle that enables the distillation of formal essence. At the highest levels of artistic creation, it works with a sympathetic and genuine vision to draw aesthetic principles onto canvas in a unique state imbued with clarity and grace.

The Second Level of Painting: the Discursive and the Spatial

The letters pressed on this page consist of straight and curved lines. We don't think of them as a visual statement, because we are used to reading their shapes as part of a code translating sound into intelligent meaning. Familiar, as we are, with their appearance and the order in which they are assembled, we recognize that the purpose of letters is to communicate an aural meaning—it would be distracting and useless to their cause, to try to see them as an aesthetic statement of shape. We don't take into account what letters are doing visually, because we are trying to gather from them information that is non-spatial—discursive. A word may conjure up an image in one's mind, but it does so through literal reference. It makes meaning in a logical, linear way: one word after another. The purpose of painting, however, is to communicate in visual, spatial terms.

On the first-level of painting we saw an overlapping of discursive and spatial elements as the artist tried to literally render the objective world around her. For the first-level artist, a still life with flowers is first and foremost an assembly of daffodils, instead of a symphony of color and shape. The first-level painter holds fast to the literal definition of the shapes confronting her. The second level artist, however, is one who consciously uses the interaction of shape, tone and color to portray the splendor and drama of life in purely visual terms.

At the second level, one begins to see the visual makeup of objects, rather then the objects themselves. The literal world becomes visual, instead of conceptual, and painting proceeds from the surface of the eyeball rather than from the frontal lobe of the brain. Instead of trying to reference a subject or make a statement of social commentary, the second-level artist puts forth a purer visual statement.

The second level artist is at once a mechanic, a composer, and a poet working from a purely visual sensibility. Having trained his eye to see the visual elements in a given subject—shape, line, value, texture and pattern, color, and edge—he presents the dynamic interplay of these elements where the first-level painter provides only the literal rendering of objects. On the second level, a painter demonstrates the mastery of the visual elements and an ability to arrange them into a harmonious and compelling relationship. The second level artist manifest a visual savvy that is rational in its approach to painting. He brings order out of the tangled visual web, rephrasing its world into a created visual reality. The primary consideration for an artist on this level is to draw forth the abstract elements from the object, and to transmute them into a purely visual construct.

The Third Level of Painting: the Intuitive

I've spent much time describing the difference between the first- and second-level painter, but when it comes to the third level, there is no way to teach it. It consists of an intuitive state of mind that has no logical entry point. It springs from within the artist and may be attained through diverse methods. Whereas the second-level effort proceeds at a more scholarly pace of methodically comparing and contrasting the how's and of why's of the visual dialog, the third level is a realm of inspiration that brings the visual elements to play in a spontaneous and automatic expression. The third-level is a magical state of mind that has no format or map to follow. It is a state of artistic enlightenment, where the artist has become at one with the visual whole.

Like the athlete who plays in "the zone," the third-level artist is synched to a vision that brings the visual event into a perfect and effortless harmony. The painting seems to complete itself. Tapping into this state of mind is not easy, because it can be neither be forced nor tamed. A visionary state of mind, which any artist of whatever talent can obtain at any given moment, the third level embodies the highest magnitude of visual awareness.

There are certain individuals who have the ability to tap into this state; some even have the ability to turn it on and off. (Think of Van Gogh's inspired output during his relatively short stay in Arles.) However, since the third level is not a fully controlled state, some have an easier ability to obtain it than others. I can lecture about what this state is about and urge you to acquire it, but in the end there is no logical doctrine that will show you how to reach it. It ultimately comes from a personal experience.

2

ACADEMIA

Let the Visual Dialogue Begin

For a new painter, a developmental course in the visual arts is about learning to control the visual elements and approaches. This is where a discerning eye and the ability to control paint are learned and applied, not as a technique, but through a comprehensive understanding of visual fundamentals. As in the study of any language, one needs to learn vocabulary and grammar before one can speak. For the student of painting, this means first acquiring knowledge of the visual dialogue. Mastering its elements and approaches is a must, in order to develop the facility to "tell" a painting in a way that is visually unique. A new painter trains to recognize and apply these principles through a process of trial and error. By applying these elements and approaches to one's own painting, the artist tests her understanding of these principles.

We are, first and foremost, visual creatures. The qualities of visual experience affect us more strongly than the other senses, and they have profound physiological impact on how we perceive and remember the world around us. Unlike the sensory experiences of taste, touch or smell, the visual experience can be closely replicated on paper, film, video, and canvas. When we re-create the visual experience on canvas, we do so with a limited yet still powerful range of light effects—visual elements and approaches—that imitate the physiological experience of sight. The second-level artist consciously develops the use of these principles. Once they become second nature, the artist can work more spontaneously, perhaps even reaching the third level.

The training of an artist is often compared to the training of an athlete, because they both involve the development of perception and physical skill sets. As an artist, your aim is to push your understanding of the visual dialogue—that interaction between shapes in a painting—and to do so in ways that enable your awareness and ability to grow. Mastering the visual elements and approaches provides a fluency in the language of the visual dialogue. This fluency is what ultimately creates great painters.

In any sport there are individual players whose mastery of the game far exceeds all others. These players may have physical gifts similar to less gifted players, but they very often seem to possess a supernatural gift to see the field of play in ways that other players can't. They may start with a similar understanding of the game, but their ability to "see" more than other players do transforms the way they play the game.

This section of the book is unabashedly left-brained in its presentation of the visual elements and approaches that comprise the fundamentals of painting. We will define and analyze these components, because they correspond to the "rules of the game," which determine the essential structure of painting. Right-brained artistic expression is comprised of something that can't be taught—that uniquely individual mixture of nature-nurture, passion and creativity that differentiates one artist's vision from another's. At first, by concentrating on the academic elements, it may feel that we're restraining that unbridled freedom of expression that we normally associate with the creative process. But this will soon change. Familiarity with these concepts breeds competence. In the long run, it will make the creative process even freer and more efficient. Don't worry: as long as you have the ability to return to your individual character, you will never become a slave to academia. Only those who lack confidence in their own point of view become imprisoned. Just keep your wits about you and test these principles against your own experience and visual sensibilities. In the end, you should come out enriched with a new-found visual literacy that will enhance your innate vision.

The Rules of the Game

Every game has an objective. In painting, the object of the game is to formulate a coherent visual dialogue. On the canvas this visual dialogue always takes place between shapes—like characters in a play. Some are major characters, some are minor. In order for this dialogue to be meaningful, these shapes need to be talking about the same concern. They need to articulate the same visual approach. Think of the visual approach as the overall theme of a painting, and think of the visual elements as the words or phrases that "shapes" use to express themselves.

A visual approach is the statement of a visual theme that identifies a particular kind of ocular experience: dark-light pattern, equalization, local tone, light and shadow, front lit—these are just a few. A visual element is one of the ways that we organize our perception of the way light interacts with the physical world. These six visual elements consist of shape line, value, texture, color, and edge. Although they all define the perception of shape, they also determine and support a visual approach. The elements are the building blocks that support the whole statement of a painting.

In order to gain a full understanding of the elements, it helps to study them along with visual approaches. Understanding how the visual elements function in a larger statement, helps to draw out their unique character and define them. As we start with a description of the six visual elements, keep in mind that, just as a painting may be characterized by one prominent visual approach—with others working to secondary effect—so a variety of visual elements can be at work in a given painting.

The Visual Elements

The six visual elements consist of *shape, line, value, texture-pattern, color,* and *edge.* As the nuts and bolts that hold together a painting's visual approach, they support and enhance each other and the whole. Your knowledge of these elements will determine your ability to shape them into a coherent visual dialogue. If you don't have control over these fundamental tools, the resulting painting will lack an organizing principle. Knowing the visual elements confers the freedom to maneuver a painting into any desired direction and facilitates the execution of a visual approach with greater confidence.

In order to understand the visual elements, let's first exaggerate their function and imagine applying them to a whole painting. For example, in order to study line as a visual element, it might be a good idea to do a painting comprised solely of lines. Imagine a painting consisting of nothing but texture, another of values only. By isolating each element, you avoid juggling the rest of the elements at the same time.

Every basketball player starts out learning the basics: dribbling, passing, shooting, and rebounding. One must learn the fundamental skills before one can play the game. Learning these skills one at a time makes the basics manageable and the game, accessible, even fun. Painting is like learning to shoot a basketball, in that many facets of this single skill-bending the knees, raising the ball, releasing the shot—come together in one fluid motion.

The visual elements function through relative relationships based on variations of quantity and quality. The character of any given element can change dramatically, depending on the surrounding elemental factors. Consider value, for example: a light value stands out more brightly when surrounded by much darker values, than it does when surrounded by values that are only slightly darker. Or color: a red mass in a field of green holds more contrast to its green complement, than it would in a field comprised of similar colors, such as purples. All visual elements exist relatively: they are defined by the elements that surround them. Therefore, in studying and applying the visual elements, it is vital to watch the effects they have on each other. This is one more reason to see the painting as a collective entity.

The Visual Approaches

A visual approach brings a sense of completion and unity to the canvas. It gives a unity of purpose and intention to the painting. It is a single visual declaration that [allows all the elements] in a painting to speak with a single voice. If a painter tries to use two approaches in the same painting, it will inevitably display confusion and a lack of commitment, as the two ideas battle for attention. It would be like carrying on two important conversations at once.

A visual approach is never clear until it applies to the whole painting. An architect, who builds on details, expecting them to hold up an edifice, isn't seeing what truly supports it. All paintings that speak with clarity do so with one voice. This makes their resulting virtue hard to ignore—regardless of authorship, price, style or public stature. There are many paintings that hang on gallery and museum walls that do not live up to this sense of visual completion. They deceive those who are unaware of the visual truth; however, to those who remain aware of the working aspects it is very evident. If there is no single visual approach, a painting's story, or visual dialogue, is confused and dissatisfying. It should be available and coherent in a single glance, yet offer an exploratory adventure that surrenders its visual riches with each further perusal. A visual approach offers a summary of the painting's story. It conveys an overall glimpse of the painting's theme, before bringing the viewer into the details of its internal dialogue. It is the dominant visual idea, an encapsulation of the visual dialogue that provides an overall direction to the painting.

Establishing a clear visual approach is of utmost importance, and in the following section we'll explore in greater depth the types of visual approaches and elements that comprise them. We start with the elements, so that you can identify them easily and learn to use them correctly. These chapters follow a logical progression that shows how related elements and approaches build on each other. In a sense, they are the hardest and most essential chapters to understand, because they build on some of the most basic tenets of perception, easily overlooked because we take them for granted.

THE VISUAL ELEMENTS

1) Shape 2) Line 3) Value 4) Texture and Pattern 5) Color 6) Edge

SHAPE

The Alpha and Omega

In order to understand how visual elements and approaches work together, we must start with the "mother of all elements and approaches"—shape. More than any visual element or approach; shape is the foundation of all painting. Visual experience cannot exist without it. It is the most basic component to creating visual meaning. All of the other visual—line, value, texture, color and edge—exist in order to define and complete shape.

Of all of the elements, shape is perhaps the hardest to conceptualize. In order to exist, a shape must be completed by one of the other elements. For example, edge and line divide space and define the shape of a mass. They are the outer skin that holds shape together, and they can be used together or separately to define shape. The other elements—value, texture and color—provide the internal character of shape. A complete shape is one that stands independently, its identity clearly defined by one value, one color and one textural statement. When you come to understand how shape is determined by the other elements and can put this principle to work on canvas, your drawing will become fluid and infuse your painting with a spontaneous precision. But first we must acquaint ourselves more thoroughly with the six visual elements and how they work together to define shape. In painting, shape is the most important expressive element, the organizing principle for everything else—the alpha and omega. A painting begins and ends with shape.

Because shape is so critical to the whole painting and to every part within it, each shape should have considerable thought behind it and reflect that level of thought by manifesting as unique and complete. Every seen object is perceived as a visual element—as shape, line, value, texture-pattern, color or edge. Whether it is empty sky or the tree branches framing that sky, these visual events are either defined as shape or create shape. For this reason, there is no such thing as "negative shape" or "negative space"; every perceived entity in our immediate field of vision holds mass and has shape, no matter what its density. In painting, it is critical to recognize that the visual elements define these shapes and not the objects that they come from. Every visual element that you introduce into your work—no matter how small or unimportant it may seem—it must complete itself as a shape.

Typically, a canvas is a single rectangular or square shape. The goal of the artist is to take that shape and break it down into an infinite number of smaller shapes, and then bring that division back into unity again. In the beginning, the blank canvas starts as one whole shape, but as soon as you make your first mark on it, you have broken that mass into an arrangement of shapes. As you keep painting, every new statement is going to affect the whole compositional breakdown. Imagine striking a porcelain plate with a hammer. With each strike, the plate is divided into smaller shapes, each fragment a part of the whole composition, the outline of which is still visible. The process of constructing a painting is similar. Even though we deconstructing the original large shape, all of those smaller shapes must relate back to the whole again, no matter how many times we strike with our hammer. Essentially every note that you make is a chip off the whole block. Ideally, each one is unique in size and shape, but all will be needed to reconstitute the plate's state of original wholeness.

One question that may be "taking shape" is what glues together all of those shapes? There are many different ways to stitch together shapes in a painting, but the main cohesive force is the Big Shape, which all successful paintings require.

Big Shape

The big shape is the underlying foundation for almost any painting. It is neither an element nor a visual approach, but is defined by one overall value relationship, or statements of value, which group together into one unit. It can be one simple shape in a single value. Either way, it forms into one defined overall shape, so that when you squint, you will see that all of its values group into a single big shape.

All successful paintings and visual approaches have a big shape that dominates the structure of the painting and holds it together with a coherent design that can be seen from across the room. The big shape brings together all of the painting's secondary shapes into one grand declaration, and does so through a unique blending of proportional relationships within the big shape. A successful break down of big shape provides a level of abstract interest that will allow a painting to work whether it's hung upside down or sideways. A well-designed big shape ties together all of the shapes in a painting, even those not contained within its mass. Turning the painting in different directions, reveals errant shapes that appear to fall off the canvas or seem weak if they are not anchored in place by the frame-work of the big shape.

In order to work with big shape, it is important to understand how to observe and see big shape abstractly. Ideally, all shapes in a painting should be connected so that they coalesce into one unifying shape. For the realistic painter, the big shape need not convey any of the subject's specific imagery, but may be assem-bled compositely by combining various images or shapes together into an abstract design. If you fight the idea of abstraction, you will struggle to get control of your painting. The big shape is a singular unit, which the viewer can easily read and which will resolve the painting from across the room—not because it literally ren-ders a given subject, but for its sense of coherent design. The immediate effect of a successfully executed big shape is similar to the image that resonates against the back of the eyes when a flash camera suddenly floods a scene with light: it renders a visual impact that organizes the image and captures the event in an infinite moment of perception.

As a painter, you are like an architect constructing visual edifices. Think of the big shape as your blueprint. A misconceived architectural blueprint will have obvious consequences when a wall collapses or a ceiling cracks; but when a paint-ing is poorly conceived, it is obvious only to those who have a trained eye. Under-standing the function of visual approach will help avoid errors. The block-in of a painting is like drafting a blueprint: once the foundational shapes are in place, it is easy to tell if the initial statement will work, provided you know what to look for.

Shape Quality

What defines good shape? Shape quality is determined by two factors: originality and completeness. A shape becomes unique when its drawing characteristics are distinctive in relation to all other shapes on the canvas. It is unique in its basic singularity. It holds an allure that defines it independently from other shapes, but not so much so that it overwhelms the whole design. A shape may make a bold and distinctive statement or it may dissolve into the subtleties of a painting, but it should never draw away attention from the whole.

If you don't know how to complete a shape, it is difficult to figure out how to draw with it. Shape is completed by the elements that form it. It is unique in how it is singularly defined in relation to the rest of the shapes around it. Nature is infinitely rich in its variety of forms which never exactly repeat themselves, yet appear bound by a unified wholeness. Every snowflake is a hexagram, yet pos-sesses a unique design within that form. This variety within a common unity appears in the products of man as well: a sonnet is composed of three quatrains and a final couplet, yet the range of meaning and imagery expressed within that form is infinite. The art in nature and man alike lies in the blending of chaos and form. Without form, snowflakes would have no shape and without variety they would be generic and dull. Chaos and order are stitched into the same quilt. A shape that possesses quality has a sense of chaos and order to it. It is structured by visual elements that are uniquely applied, but integrated into the whole. A big shape will provide the foundational skeleton that unifies a painting's underlying structure, but integration will bring a unified appeal to the whole. By integrating every new element and idea, you can keep adding uniqueness to a painting without losing unity.

Generic vs. Unique Properties

A generic shape is one comprised of an equal order of its components. If snowflakes were only about order, they all would look alike and not vary in pattern or size. A square is generic in the precise equability of its angles and dimensions. It lacks the interest of uniqueness or the chaos of diversity. A painting composed of generic shapes will create a dry and stale impression. A square shape that departs from the norm and offers variation in its angles and dimensions is still held together by form, yet offers a simultaneous sense of variety. Is it then easier to draw geometric shapes or random shapes that are more organic in nature? Actually, it may be easier in some ways to work with more organic shapes, because they have more freedom to change than shapes that are geometric in nature. However, organic shapes can be more difficult to control because of their chaotic nature.

Creating unique shape is always more difficult, but it can be done with the right persistence and awareness. A good shape should never be equal in its drawing and relationship to the rest of the shapes in a painting. It should possess an original charm and strength of character. A shape's quality depends on originality and on its completion by one of the other visual elements. If you study shapes in nature, you will find that they consist of visual elements that are never totally equal. Attached as we are to our capacity for reason, human beings like to put things into equal order. As artists, we often make the mistake of indulging this impulse in our paintings, when, in reality, we should be trying to engage the spontaneous visual dialogue of order and chaos that exists in nature. To be a visual painter, you must become a visual narrator of life and nature.

Shape Harmony

Shape harmony is one way to bring more unity into a painting, but should be thought out thoroughly, since it is not a visual situation that exists naturally. Harmony is created by disposing a visual element throughout a painting in a way that uses shared features or characteristics to bind the composition within a set of common formal motifs. To create shape harmony, take three shapes characteristics—a shape characteristic is not a whole shape in itself, but one of its distinguishable traits—and use them to define and form all of the shapes in your painting. You are not creating three different shapes, but creating many new shapes from three uniquely defined characteristics. These can be square, organic, jagged, and so on; however, what is needed are three separate traits that are specific enough in their character so that they can form new diverse shapes. In bringing about a shape harmony, you want to convey a uniformity to all shapes, while retaining their uniqueness. You should end up with many different looking shapes, but since they all are designed from three variable traits, they will be harmonized compositionally. You are forming a companionship between all shapes so that they will look as if they sprang from the same root, or were born from the same mother.

Painters of many different eras and styles have applied shape harmony to their works: El Greco, de Kooning, Charles Burchfield, Van Gogh, Albert Ryder, Thomas Benton, and Georgia O'Keefe. They are all noted for maintaining a play of shape harmony in their works for most of their careers.

LINE

No matter how thick or thin it is, a line has no mass or shape. By definition, it inscribes a boundary between shapes. Like edge, a line gives space its shape. In one sense, there is no drawing to a line; it merely traces the edge of a mass. Conceptually, line has no mass or shape, no matter how thick or thin it becomes. It exists purely to demarcate adjacent masses. If there were drawing to a line, it would become a shape. What differentiates a line from a shape is the uniform length of its width. When you create a line, you must pay attention to the shapes that it creates on both sides of the line. One line simultaneously draws two shapes.

As a visual element, line separates shapes more decisively than edge. Edge determines how the shape of a mass completes itself and relates to an adjacent mass. Edge may consist of softening of the shape so that it blends almost seamlessly with the shape next to it, or it may form a hard statement that causes it to butt up against the neighboring shape. Line, however, has a more abstract feel to it, because most of what we see and observe in the real world is divided by edge and not by line. Line is an intellectual concept that imposes a demarcation between objects or shapes that is not always so clearly defined in nature. Because it doesn't exist naturally, line often must be pushed in the creative process. You often must make a conscious choice to use line as a visual element. Since line does not occur naturally in the physical world, realists seeking a literal rendering of visual reality will rarely use it as an element.

VALUE

Value is a measure of lightness or darkness, and every shape that you create retains a value. Every color also has value, though color, as its own visual element has no effect on value. Color intensity can be deceptive in its relationship to its corresponding value. For example, a bright red appears to be light in value, because of its high intensity of color; actually, its value is quite dark in tone. Value pertains only to the tonal shade of a shape. It is what really defines the internal structure of a shape and gives color and texture a platform to stand on. Value defines shape in the absence of line, and ultimately is responsible for creating the big shape in any given painting. In this sense, painting is mainly about the use of value relationships to establish shape. This is why it is rarely necessary to sketch linear shapes on canvas to start a painting; it is more useful and faster to block in the design using value. Drawing with values, rather than line, provides a more interactive and natural approach, to putting paint on canvas.

Value Harmony: High and Low key

High key or low key painting refers to the grouping of values either at the light or dark end of the tonal spectrum. A high key painting uses light values and appears light overall, whereas a low key painting uses a darker range of values, so that the painting appears more somber. In either case, you skew the tonal values to an extreme. The ensuing harmony derives from the congruent arrangement of values, which unifies the painting's tone. A high key value placement compares to the tonal range of a photographic print resulting from an over-exposed negative: the values are grouped near the light end of the spectrum. A low-key painting corresponds to under-exposure: the resulting image retains its value organization, but is darker. Assuming a value scale from one to ten, with one being white and ten, black—a high key painting would locate its values between one and four, while a low key would range from seven to ten. A high or low-key value state-ment applies to the whole painting, and it can work with any visual approach. Whether you paint in high or low key, the difficulty lies in retaining the value structure of the painting.

COLOR

After exploring color extensively for the last few years, I find that I have become somewhat of a colorist. Yet, having said that and although there is much to know about color theory and the ways color interact on canvas, value still will always remain more important—simply because it provides the underlying structure of a painting. In spite of its infinite complexity, color remains merely an element that stains the foundation of value tones. It is a filter laid over the top of value. If you structure a painting with a rich array of values, your colors will appear rich too. If you apply the worst color relationships imaginable, a painting will still hold up, providing its values are well-conceived. However, not even the best color rela-tionships can survive a weak array of tonal values. Making both elements work well is best, but value will always provide the key foundation.

One of the most difficult but most intriguing aspects to painting is its relative nature. A color always relates to the colors around it, and that relationship in turn affects the whole canvas. That's why, when talking about color, the suffix "-ish" is a helpful addition to each designation of color. By appending an "-ish" to the end of your color, you remind yourself of that color's relative nature.

For example, say you put down your first color note on a blank canvas—a yel-lowish green. It is immediately evident what color it is. But, next, you place a red-dish orange next to it, and suddenly both colors look different than they would have, had they been applied alone. The yellowish green appears greener, and the reddish orange looks even redder, due to their complementary relationship, which we will explore shortly. Your next color—a violet—even further compli-cates the plot. The violet remains somewhat unchanged, because it is balanced by the yellow green and reddish orange—again the complementary influ-ence—though it may appear a bit warmer. But notice that the yellowish green now becomes more yellow, and the reddish orange becomes more orange. The more colors that you add, the more it will change the color relationships—some-times for better, sometimes for worse. You can make even the worst muck beauti-ful, if you apply it next to the right color group. A color that doesn't work fails due to its poor relationship to the colors around it, not by its own merits. For that reason, there is no such thing as a bad color, only bad color relationships. Adding the "-ish" will keep this principle firmly in mind.

The relativity of color can be overwhelming, and artists have developed various strategies for dealing with its challenges. Tonalists—like Sargent, Pollock, and Wyeth—kept their colors subdued so as to emphasize value. Colorists—like Sorolla, de Kooning, and Monet—brought the dynamic allure of color to the forefront. There are numerous color theories, based on a variety of prominent color relationships, but before we explore these concepts there is one point that needs to be addressed: color temperature. The warmth or coolness of a color is a relative characteristic that occurs automatically in the course of working out a color arrangement. Although it can be a useful descriptive term, color temperature must be kept in its relative context. For example, red is typically considered a "warm" color and green is labeled "cool." But yellow green will be warm compared to a blue green. Both are considered cool in the objective scheme, but in this context the temperature of each is relative. Temperature is always determined by color relationship, so if you pay attention to the way one color influences and plays off of another, you will be paying attention to the temperature as well. When taken out of the context of color relationship, the notion of temperature is too vague. If you base your assessment of color on fixed ideas of warmth or coolness, you'll be confused. Think in terms of color relationships and avoid making objective measures of temperature.

Color Theory: The Triads

Light consists of energy waves that are grouped together in a continuous range, or spectrum. Light that appears white, such as light from the sun, is, in fact, made up of many colors that interact simultaneously. Although the wavelengths of light have no color, they do produce the sensation of color.

The wavelengths detectible to the human eye represent just a small segment of the electromagnetic energy spectrum—the visible light spectrum. The short wavelengths at the end of the visible light spectrum are perceived as blue. The longer wavelengths at the other end of the visible spectrum are seen as red. All the other colors perceptible in nature are found along the spectrum between blue and red. (Beyond the limits of the visible spectrum, the short wavelengths of ultraviolet light and X-rays and the long infrared and radio wavelengths are invisible to the human eye.)

A glass prism divides the visible spectrum of light into its primary colors, and when that array of colors is arranged in a circle it creates a color wheel. The color wheel is anchored by the three primary colors—red, blue and yellow—each of which corresponds to one of the three points of an equilateral triangle overlaying the cover wheel. The colors resulting from the combination of each pairing of primaries forms another grouping called the secondary triad—orange, purple, and green. The primary and secondary triads are separate groupings of colors with very different harmonies. The colors of the primary triad work in relative harmony with each other, and the colors of the secondary triad provide an entirely different set of concordant statements. You need promote only one of the two triads in any given painting to establish an innate sense of color relationship.

The range of color variations within each triad is quite vast, especially when you apply an "-ish" to the color choices you've chosen to address your shapes. For example, a reddish, blueish, or yellowish hue can neutralize to almost any gray or brown, as long as it still reads as one of the three defining colors within the primary triad. The secondary triad works along the same lines. You can mix an array of interesting grays by combining the colors of the secondary triad. For example, green + orange + purple = a concord gray.

The Complements

Colors that are diametrically opposed on the color wheel are called complements and bear a strong contrasting relationship to one another. For example, the complement to yellow is purple, which resides opposite yellow on the color wheel. The three main complementary dyads, or pairings, are blue-orange, red-green, and yellow-purple. Any one of these dyads will bring a dynamic color relationship to a canvas. In a painting composed of reddish and greenish tints, the eye finds coherent contrast and order. Once again, you can mix wonderful grays by blending complements. For example, red + green = a concord gray.

The Complement Test

Color theory relates to the color arrangement of a painting—that statement of hues which renders a unifying color code and provides either a satisfying sense of harmony or contrast. Contrast creates an activating response in the viewer. Harmony is more calming in its effect. Complementary color theory is based on our physiological perception of color. A simple experiment demonstrates the complementary principle as it is built into our ocular experience of color. The test requires a white sheet of paper and a pack of color paper. Lay the white sheet of paper down on a table and place a smaller piece of colored paper on top of it. Focus on the colored paper for 30 to 60 seconds, and then remove the colored paper without losing your focus on the white sheet. For a moment you will see on the white sheet a clear afterimage of the color's complement. The eye appears to seek its complement to neutralize the effect of over-stimulation. It is also interesting to see what happens when you combine two colored papers in this test.

Analogous & Split-Complementary Color Schemes

The analogous scheme uses a dominant group of colors situated close together on the color wheel. Because all of the colors come from the same area of the color wheel, the resulting scheme creates a harmonious color grouping. The split complementary adds variety and depth, to this scheme by using analogous colors in opposition to a subordinate complementary array, with an even smaller presence of accented discords. For example, let's say your group dominant colors span a range of yellow to orange. To that major array of colors in yellow-orange and orange-yellow, you add a smaller grouping of complementaries. Blues work particularly well because they complement the dominant oranges. You then include the discordant accents—purple and green—in smaller amounts than the blue. Green and purple will work because they are compatible with orange—all three being the colors of the secondary triad.

The proportion of the colors is critical in getting this theory to work. In our example, the yellow-oranges and oranges have the largest presence, followed by the blues, which are complementary, and then the accented discords which take up even less space then the blue. The reason for this unequal weighting of color is to emphasize the overall complementary theory (orange-blue), and to subordinate the accented statement of the secondary triad. The complementary scheme dominates the secondary triad. As you can tell, this scheme arrangement uses two schemes at once, and requires a good understanding of basic theory to execute it.

Contrast of Saturation

Contrast of saturation may be applied to any color scheme, by juxtaposing grays and saturated colors in uneven quantities. For example, if you dominate with grays, you juxtapose those grays with small amounts of saturated color. If you dominate with saturated colors, you juxtapose with small amounts of gray. In either case, the small amount of contrasting saturation will stand out. Andrew Wyeth frequently uses neutralized colors that are accented by small color notes in more intense hues.

Color Harmony

Color harmony is not a color theory, per se, but a way to unify color. Like shape harmony, it is not a visual approach, but just another way to bring unity to a painting. Color harmony is perhaps the easiest way to solve a color problem or to unify a painting. It requires taking one color and making that the "mother color" for all of the colors in the painting. Essentially, you are dipping a bit of the mother color into every color involved in the painting, but you need to add enough of it so each one reflects the mother color. If the mother color is orange, you would mix that color into all of the colors used in the painting, so that in the end all of your colors resonate with that one foundational color note.

A word of caution about color harmony: don't confuse it with color as a visual approach. Though they are somewhat close in concept, they are vary in execution and their final effect. Color harmony ties many different colors together with one color, whereas color as a visual approach is about stating the variety of one color within a painting.

TEXTURE & PATTERN

Texture and pattern refers both to the surface of a subject portrayed in a painting and to the application of paint across the surface of the canvas—its paint quality. As an element, texture and pattern derive from the visual approach of equalization, in which a form is repeated within a shape to suggest a sense of texture or rhythm. As a visual element, texture expresses the surface quality of a shape, while pattern has a more rhythmic component to it. Texture reveals the tactile effect or characteristic feel of a surface, be it fur, grass, asphalt or baby fat. Each has a textural quality that defines its surface. These textures may be used out of their subjective contexts to provide new experiences of the interaction of shapes and textures in a painting.

Paint quality—the relative thickness and texture of paint application—can be equally expressive as a visual element and dramatically affects color and shape dynamics. As a visual expression of the surface quality, or feel, of a subject, texture often makes use of pattern to create its effects. Pattern uses the repetition of shapes to provide a uniform design with a rhythmic character to it. Patterns exist in wallpaper, fabrics, the stripes of zebras, the scales of fish, patches of clouds, and so on. A pattern effect always derives from a design based on recurring shapes.

EDGE

Edge is most often defined by value, although color and texture can do the job as well. Typically, value creates the edge in a painting's big shape, but within that big shape there can be numerous smaller shapes defined by color, texture, or slight value shifts, all of which require an edge to give them definition. The great-est contrast will usually be found in the edge surrounding the big shape. Edge forms the perimeter of shape, the boundary where the shape-defining elements of color, texture or value meet an adjoining shape, which, in turn, is defined by con-trasting color, texture or value.

The difference between line and edge is that line can define the boundary between two shapes consisting of identical value, texture or color, whereas edge cannot. Edge requires contrast between adjacent shapes: a change in one, if not all three, of the internal visual elements—value, texture and color—that exists in two contiguous shapes. As an artist, it requires the utmost attention to see the edge form and then to use it in order to draw out the intended shape. Shape qual-ity is a function of the artist's awareness of unique form and the competing inter-nal visual elements (value, texture and color) that give the shape its quality. When drawing with line, an artist may isolate an individual shape and ignore its internal elements; however, when drawing with edge, the artist must see two contiguous shapes simultaneously, and use their internal visual elements to differentiate them.

Edge is an effective tool for blending or separating contiguous shapes. As the boundary between shapes, an edge acts like a fence, which may be tall and intim-idating, or low and more accessible. Edges come in a full variety of sharpness and softness. A sharp, bold edge works like a solid brick fence: it restrains the eye and confines it within a given shape. A soft edge allows movement and greater access to a neighboring shape. When an edge is completely annihilated, it allows the eye to freely access an adjacent shape.

Since edge is what holds together shape, it needs to be clearly defined in the artist's mind even though parts of it may be softened or understated in the final painting. A painter may soften an edge to near extinction, but it should never lose its underlying graphic value. A *graphic* shape is one that retains sharp edges. Start-ing with graphic shapes establishes them more precisely, enabling you to under-stand their unique qualities and how they relate to their neighbors. At the beginning of a painting, graphic rendering clarifies shape. An *atmospheric* shape consists mainly of soft edges. Even if your shapes start out looking atmospheric, they should derive from an underlying sense of graphic design. If you start with a soft-edged shape you are almost always stuck with it, because it is hard to get it back to a sharper stage. However, if you start out with a graphic shape, it is easy to soften its edges. By starting from a point of design clarity, you will have an eas-ier time in controlling the overall shape quality of your work.

Value and Edge

Edge quality describes the relative sharpness or softness of a shape's boundary, in comparison to the other edges in a painting. There can be a wide range of edge qualities in a painting, and many different ways to create those edges. As we have seen, a painting's sharpest edge occurs at the site of its greatest contrast, and in most paintings the greatest contrast delineates the big shape. On the other hand, when a painting's values are close in tone, the corresponding edges appear softer, more atmospheric, even though they have not been physically manipulated, or smudged. The closer the values of two adjoining shapes, the softer their edges will appear. With that said, when it does come to smudging an edge, it can be done anywhere on the canvas, even where the value contrast is at its highest.

Affecting the Edge

Once you establish an edge between shapes, you can soften it either by painting in a value-, texture-, or color change in one of the shapes, or by smudging the existing edge. For example, in painting a soft edge using value, you would apply a value that is only slightly different in tone from the value in the adjacent shape. A slightly different color or texture would accomplish the same effect. Through this graphic application, you close the value, textural or color range between two adjoining shapes and create an atmospheric effect. The other way to affect an edge is to do so by manipulating it through a wet-on-wet application, wherein you paint in the sharp edge first, and then smudge it with a brush, thumb, or rag, in order to soften it. Putting in the sharp edge first establishes the shapes, so that when you smudge the edge you change only its quality.

There are many reasons to manipulate an edge. You may soften an edge in order to create a passage between shapes and join them together, or you might repeat a soft edge to create rhythm throughout the big shape. You might use a gradation of edge from hard to soft in order to add depth. There are many reasons to affect an edge, but they should always enhance the visual story that your painting is trying to tell.

One technique that encourages a greater variety of edge in a painting is to compose a big shape with only three sharp edges. If done correctly, the three edges will play off of one another and unify the big shape. The three sharp edges should inscribe design components that are different from each other, yet strategically placed to accent the big shape. Beyond that, how you get these edge elements to work is up to you. But remember: for edge to work most effectively, all the other elements in the painting should be complete. That means building interesting shapes through a dynamic variety of value, texture, color and line. Edge works best when all the other elements are clearly established.

Atmospheric and Graphic

When it comes to edge, there are two kinds of painters: atmospheric or graphic. It really does not make any significant difference into which category you fit. A painter who loses a lot of edges will create an atmospheric feel in their works—Rembrandt and Monet are two good examples of atmospheric painters. On the other hand, a graphic painter is one who uses many sharp edges—Van Gogh and Georgia O'Keefe. A master painter can be either one, but which style emerges depends on that ineffable blend of training, instinct and taste that we call the creative process.

GRADATION and HARMONY

Gradation and Harmony are qualities that don't quite fit into either category: visual elements or visual approaches. However, as techniques that can work well with a variety of approaches, they can strongly affect the visual dialogue, and so probably require separate discussion. They are not as fundamental as big shape, so they are not always needed, but they are statements that can add movement or unity to the surface of the canvas.

Gradation is an attribute of directional movement that can be introduced into all visual approaches. It can inflect a visual element with a sense of direct movement from top to bottom, bottom to top, or side to side. For example, a value that shifts from light to dark as it moves horizontally across the canvas creates a directional pull. Any of the six elements can take on a gradation and do so in a variety of ways: busy to quiet textures, cool to warm colors, large to small shapes.

Gradation may be applied within a single shape, to create movement within that shape and to lead the eye to another adjacent shape; or it can be applied to the whole painting, in order to unify the whole statement of a painting.

Harmony

Like gradation, harmony is a technique that provides accompaniment to a specific visual element by unifying its characteristics across the whole canvas. It enhances the individual character of the elements' components while uniting them as one. Shape, color, value and pattern lend themselves to harmony more easily than line or edge, because these elements fill in [the content of] a shape, whereas line and edge are more suited to define the boundaries of shape. Value harmony may be as simple as stating a painting in a high or low tonal key. Color and shape harmony each has its own character, [based on a repetition of the key element]. Harmony is used to unify the painting's surface, but it is not required—and sometimes a mix of contrasting elements can make an even more effective statement.

CONCLUSION

Understanding the visual elements provides the tools to enhance a painting by helping to clarify its visual approach. Like parts of speech—nouns, verbs and adjectives—the elements combine into a visual dialogue that characterize a painting's visual approach. If you lack an understanding of the elements and how they relate to a painting's visual approach, your painting will struggle to make a coherent statement. This book is designed to introduce the visual elements and approaches simultaneously, so you can begin to see how they work together. As you digest this material and work with the various elements to refine your visual approach, don't neglect your drawing skills. Shape is the keystone of visual elements. It organizes all the others and determines the coherence of your visual approach. To create interesting shapes, you need to be able to render what you see in reality and in your mind's eye. To draw well, you must see well and you must possess the eye-hand coordination to transpose that vision onto canvas. This is particularly critical to painting, where the dominant shape and its proportions form the foundation of the work and go a long way to determining its success or failure.

THE VISUAL APPROACHES

1) Shape 2) Line 3) Dark-light Pattern 4) Equalization 5) Local Tone 6) Form 7) Light & Shadow 8) Silhouette 9) Frontal Light 10) Color 11) Edge

A good painting ought to abound with a sense of unity, and it is the visual approach that brings this about. A visual approach gives a purpose or theme to a painting and is the subject that the painting addresses in its entirety. Each of the visual approaches is like a singular moment or first impression. When all of a painting's shapes and elements come together to reinforce the statement of its visual approach, the resulting effect creates an image of dynamic clarity and impact.

I can define and describe the various visual approaches, but how you apply them is unformulated, in that there is no one right way to realize them. They each embody a distinct logic that differentiates them from one another, yet they remain relative in nature. It is up to you to get them to work, and to state them in your own style.

There are eleven visual approaches, or thematic statements, that may be applied to a given painting. Each of the six of the visual elements constitutes a separate visual approach, and in addition to those there are five more that are not elements. Each one constitutes a statement that brings about a visual coherence to a painting.

SHAPE

As a visual approach, shape provides the central theme of a painting. A difficult approach to work with, it requires a great deal of understanding of how shape works on a purely abstract level. As we saw in our discussion of the visual elements, the whole painting must first speak about shape before it engages the other elements. Shape focuses the breakdown and relationship of space. There are very few painters in history who have painted works using this visual approach. Two who pushed this approach considerably are El Greco and de Kooning. Though there work was executed centuries apart and is quite different in style, the two artists are related by their emphasis on pure shape quality.

El Greco's painting *The Burial of Count Orgaz* is a good example of shape as a visual approach. The shapes are defined by edge and value. If you look to the shapes revealed by El Greco's handling of values—and not to the imagery involved—you will see the true organization of the painting. The orchestration of shapes reveal a visual story, aside from the literal imagery, which disclose the painting's true nature. The shapes conform to an underlying sense of harmony in the painting. They work with each other to support the whole visual idea of shape. Most remarkable about this painting is the overall gradation of shape in a progression from top to bottom, comprised of forms that move from small to large. This gradation, along with the emphasis of shape, unites the painting into one grand celebration of shape.

LINE

As a visual approach, line becomes the dominant statement that defines shapes through the painting. Typically, when line is used as an element to define shape, it generally is combined with other approaches. However, when it is promoted throughout the painting, and unites the canvas into one whole statement, it becomes a visual approach. More often, value is used to define shape by creating the edge that separates shapes. However, when line is used as a visual approach, value and edge are replaced by line to define and separate shapes. To use line effectively, the value of the painting's surface should consist mainly of one value statement. If you combine value with line as the main visual approach, it detracts from how the shape quality is defined, because value and edge will work against line as a defining element. So the painting must be in one tone to allow line to do its work. Without value to define shape, there are no edges to provide separation between shapes, leaving a clear field for line to define, draw and separate shapes. Line divides space with a randomized exertion of shape completion. This means that no two lines or shapes are ever repeated. Each line is expressed uniquely in order to define unique shapes. The resulting work displays a randomness to the completion of line and shape, which appear to speak together as if with one breath.

Artist such as Egon Schiele and Franis Kline used line as a visual approach in much of their work, but no one proclaimed its qualities more eloquently than Willem de Kooning in his painting *Excavation*. If you are unaware of the visual components that went into this painting, you can never truly appreciate its mastery. The painting is the size of a barn door, and when you stand in its presence you feel enveloped by its atmosphere. Consisting of a welter of shapes and lines arranged in random arrangement, no two of the painting's markings are equal. De Kooning's lines always present a different thickness and length, while completing the shape's features with a unique and passionate expression. Astonishing expression and originality reside in each line and shape, as well as in the application of paint. The canvas is complete both technically and emotionally. Far from trying to render a picturesque scene, de Kooning interprets shape relationship with a dynamic and organic force that speaks more about realism than most literate renderings ever could. *Excavation* possesses an unpredictable originality, that is both powerful yet thoughtful in its sophistication. De Kooning's intent was not to trace real-world imagery, but to conform shape and line to a sense of organic spontaneity that captures the inimitable power of nature. He uses line to contain shape, but where those lines break, they allow shapes to interlock. He leads the eye from one form to the next, until, eventually, he has stitched together all the shapes into a surface of enigmatic unity. It is hard not to get caught up in the profound sense of tranquil efflorescence that radiates from the painting's surface.

DARK-LIGHT PATTERN

Dark-Light Pattern is a visual approach based on the interaction of two large shapes, defined by a strong, consistent value difference, with one shape emerging as the dominant statement. Because it uses only two values, dark-light pattern paintings can appear to be abstract. Dark-light pattern is not a visual approach about abstraction, *per se*, but an approach that is applied abstractly. It may be representational or fully abstract in style, but its essentials are abstract, based primarily on the interaction of shape. Dark-light pattern reduces the space of the canvas to two values, or two whole shapes, one value that is dark, and the other, light. The dark shape divides and draws the light shapes, and the light shapes divide and draw out the dark shapes. The result is a positive break down removing the suggestion of negative space. The proportion between light and dark shapes is never fifty-fifty, because that would prevent one of the two shapes from making a dominant statement. A fifty-fifty breakdown would give the effect of a checkerboard, demanding equal attention from both shapes and causing the eye to go back and forth without settling on one statement. Having one of the two shapes dominate proportionally allows that shape to speak more loudly and gives the painting focus.

The dark-light pattern painting should read as one whole configuration of either the light or the dark, and it is that completion of pattern that brings unity to the painting. The resulting pattern should render a network of shapes that are entwined in their design. They should hold together as if connected by the same thread that winds through the painting, like water coursing through a stream.

The shapes should appear to be joined into a single entity, in a manner suggesting that if you were to lift one of its interior shapes off the canvas the rest would tug along with it. The resulting pattern may be a dominate shape, as in Robert Motherwell's *Elegy to the Spanish Repulic#34,* or it can be a smaller pattern within the dominate shape, as in Andrew Wyeth's *Wolf Moon.* Both paintings are good examples of dark-light pattern. Other outstanding examples to consider are Jack Levine's *The Turnkey* and *Birmingham '63* as well as Albert Ryder's *Death on a Pale Horse* and *Moonlight Marine.*

Egon Schiele's *Sunflower* is one more painting that convincingly captures this visual approach. The dark sunflower dominates the painting, its enclosed pattern revealed as a single shape standing vertically in one moving unit. The shapes within the sunflower draw the eye upward through a procession of patterns, each shape within diversely and elegantly drawn in all of its qualities. Starting at the base of the flower, attention is pulled upwards, mounting the stem to the two large leaves, which, in turn, propel the eye to the topmost shape of the flower pattern, and then down again. The overall design transmits a sense of movement from shape to shape, yet conveys a sense of unity within the large sunflower shape. It feels as if you peeled off a single shape, the whole flower would come off the canvas as one.

EQUALIZATION

Equalization is a visual approach that brings a uniform sense of pattern to a painting's surface. The intent is to depict a uniform pattern and rhythm, so that the entire canvas becomes the focus. An equalized painting requires that the artist exerts even amounts of each visual element introduced into the painting, but does so in a manner that is constantly varied. An equalized painting, therefore, is never exactly equal in all of its aspects, just equal in its entirety. The idea is to render an equalized arrangement of parts that are filled with infinite variety.

In an equalized painting all of the shapes are similar in proportion, thus creating a sense of rhythmic pattern. The canvas conveys an evenness of surface, yet the shapes remain diverse in their characteristic features. All of the painting's elements are emphasized equally, yet still retain a distinctive quality. For example, if you place a cad-red medium in an equalized painting, you would repeat its statement in similar proportion, evenly spaced throughout the painting, while retaining the unique and distinct drawing quality of each red shape.

An equalized painting typically consists of three statements, each of which is identified by a consistent value statement, shape and pattern. Each pattern conveys a different type of movement. When the painting's elements are combined, they form one intricate movement that provides the painting's sense of unity. Each of the three statements within the larger pattern is made up of one value statement of a light, medium, or dark. Just as every good painting should avoid exactly equal proportions and relationships, equalization introduces its three patterns so that each is uniquely defined. Each pattern holds a distinctive design that differentiates it from the other two, each of the three bearing a dissimilar proportional relationship, and each unique in its spatial relationship from one another. It is still best to have one pattern or set of shapes dominate the painting, so that one of the patterns speaks more loudly in creating the visual dialogue.

It is possible to break down an equalized painting into two statements. The resulting interaction would suggest a light-and-shadow approach instead of a dark-light pattern. A dark-light pattern would contradict the whole approach, because the equalized statements would compete for dominance. An equalized light and shadow approach can be found in a situation where the light shape itself is equally distributed through the design. A row of objects—cars, bottles, cans, houses—might reflect this equal distribution into a pattern of light and shadow. To begin with, it may be easier to think of equalization working in three whole values or shapes.

Jackson Pollock's best known work—his drip paintings—embody equalization as a visual approach. The difference between splashing paint and Pollock's measured approach lies in his understanding of equalization. In order to see how he developed the drip paintings, it is useful to examine the precedent set in his earlier works, in which he drew in rhythmic patterns comprised of smaller shapes. In his 1943 painting *Mural*, Pollock created a patterned canvas from shapes rendered in three values. The main dark pattern moves across the painting in one continuous motion. Each of its internal black shapes are uniquely rendered, yet all work together to create a harmonious movement across the canvas. The same is true with the light pattern, which takes on a different feel as it swirls around the dark statement in a contrasting motion, each of its internal shapes offering a unique statement within the larger light form. The medium value is grayish blue; and while it creates its own pattern too, it is tied to the dark pattern by its value relationship. Each pattern is defined by its own shape and value quality, yet all three patterns come together to form one sinuous interwoven movement. Pollack's later drip paintings build on this same harmony of disparate values and shapes. However, instead of painting in his lexicon of shapes and patterns with a brush, he slashed and dripped them onto the canvas. He would toss down the paint in one manner for the dark statement. He would then lay down the gray with a different effect, and finally he would splash down the lights in still another. Although the three treatments retain their own integrity, they unify into one equalized homogeneous statement with a sense of depth, texture and rhythm never before seen.

LOCAL TONE

Local tone is a visual approach that condenses value into three groups: light, medium and dark, with one group predominating over the other two. The phrase "local tone" refers to a summary value statement that can occur within the whole scene or within major shapes within the scene. The overall effect of a local tone approach is similar to the value relationships that occur on an overcast day, when there is no direct sunlight to divide the landscape into light and shadow. Without cast shadows, the value arrangement of a given scene consists of the intrinsic lights and darks of the objects within that scene. Without the intensifying effects of light and shadow, the values flatten, thus compressing the gradation of lights and darks—gradation referring to the movement of light across the scene.

Typically, in a local tone approach, the scene is broken down into three fundamental value groups. These groupings are decided by the predominant relationships between values, which link tones close in value link into a single grouping. Physiologically, this grouping occurs naturally as the pupil dilates to accommodate different light intensity. When focusing on a dark subject within a fully lit scene, the pupil opens and the eye groups the brighter values together. Squinting creates the same effect, grouping close values together.

To study the value groupings within a local tone setting, the florescent lighting in a super market provides a good environment, because the diffuse overhead lights filter out most of the shadow masses. Bathed in a diffused light source that comes from all directions, all of the values in the supermarket scene will form into three groups. After a moment, you may also notice that the three groupings then condense into two primary categories of a light and dark. As the values form into two large groups, the medium value grouping will connect to either the light or dark group. If the medium value is in close range to the light grouping, then it will appear more connected to the lights, making the dark grouping stand out even more. But if the medium value grouping is relatively dark, it will tie itself to the dark value group and the light values will stand out.

Learning to see the three overall value groups or shapes is a prerequisite for bringing visual order to a given scene. If you reproduce the scene literally, value for value, you are not separating the values into groups. As you come to understand the reason for grouping the values, you can creatively render the scene's visual story in a way that is more graphically compelling. As with all visual approaches, a uniform value statement brings a static quality to the canvas and kills the visual dialogue. (This is also when you use the same amount of detail across the canvas, which ultimately happens when you slavishly copy a subject.) If you paint the scene's values as they are without adjusting them into groups, you are not interpreting the subject. When grouping values, remember that any one of the three groups can hold more than one value, but the grouping with the most values will draw the greatest focus. Structure your groupings, so that the center of interest or main shape holds the greatest variety of values. For example, to emphasize a dark value grouping, you may isolate ten or more dark values, compared to the medium and light groupings in which you would not want more than two or three values each. What defines each group is its relative separation of values. To effectively tell your visual story, keep the basic groupings as simple as possible.

Avoid applying an equal number of values to each grouping, for example five value shifts each of light, medium, and dark. Equal amounts of interest in each grouping flatten the visual dialogue. In organizing your value groups, make that your selections are unique and that they translate the scene in an engaging way. For example, you might limit your light value grouping to one value, pushing down your mid-values so they tie to the dark group in five different value shifts, and define the dark grouping in two value shifts. The fact that you are assembling the value groups in a unique and different manner adds creative tension. The visual story of value relationships adds richness to the composition. Think of the process as similar to that of piecing together the fragments of a stained glass window, or quilt, sorting the value arrangements into diverse groupings.

Local tone is over six hundred years old. Pieter Bruegel the Elder, and Hieronymus Bosch both worked with this visual approach. In Bruegel's painting *The Wedding*, the values are flattened down into a graphic composition that looks as if it had been cut from sheets of paper. Bruegel links the medium value statement to the darks, thus accentuating the light values in a way that enhances their circular pattern surrounding the table. On closer inspection, the value grouping of the light shapes reveal only two value shifts within, though multiple value shifts occur within the dark grouping, and only one value shift in the linked medium grouping. The resulting effect is a complex and enriching range of values in the dark and medium groupings, which brings out the contrast of the lights to establish a simple yet compelling design.

Over the centuries, a plethora of artists have dealt with local tone. Some, like Van Gogh and Milton Avery, spent their entire lives working in this visual approach, while others, like Sargent and Wyeth, dipped in and out of it. There are many good examples of local tone paintings to study.

FORM

Form is a property of local tone that gives dimension and a rounded feel to shape. It is a tool that may be applied to part of the canvas, for effect, or it may be applied consistently throughout a painting to provide the primary visual statement. Form is often mistaken to be a property of light and shadow, when, in fact, there are subtle but significant differences between form as applied in light and shadow and form used in local tone. The key to those differences lies in understanding how the values are held together and organized in each visual approach.

Form within light and shadow is created out of a high-contrast range of values that emphasize the shadow forms at the edges of shapes, and present a different set of rules than those defining the more diffuse light effects of local tone. In local tone, form renders the dimensionality of shape by lightening values down the middle of a shape and darkening those towards its edges in a controlled manner. In this manner, the shape does not lose its overall value statement in relation to other groupings. If the value applied begins to fight or unite with one of the other groups, it will lose the integrity of its value statement. The form's value should retain its tone within its distinctive grouping. Adding form to a local tone painting should never break up the main value relationships.

One artist who masterfully applied form to local tone paintings was Mary Cassatt. Her forms always make sense and work well with the value relationships of her paintings. Typically, Cassatt introduces form only within the light value shapes, yet the form never becomes so light or dark that it breaks through its defining value range. One can always read the value notes of the shapes to which she is applying form. By applying form only to those shapes within the light value range, Cassatt makes those forms stand out against the flatter medium and dark values, and strongly engages the viewer in the painting's visual drama.

In order to understand form as a visual approach, think of using it alone to define shape. If value is no longer the primary tool for defining shape, the artist must rely on edge. One good example of this is O'Keefe's 1927 painting *Pink Sweet Peas*, in which the painting's masses are defined not by relative values, but are shaped solely by edge and form. Some value changes remains around the edges, but they do not constitute the primary structural design. Instead, the form within each shape is created by dividing the mass's values in half. The lighter value that runs down the middle of the form does not have a characteristic shape, but is applied consistently to all the forms in the painting, suggesting the modeling effect of the light. Malevich Kasimir is another artist who used form extensively as a visual approach in his work. Form is what creates the dominant shapes and ultimately defines the visual statement.

LIGHT-AND-SHADOW

Light-and-shadow is a visual approach that is broken down into two value statements—one light and one dark—much the way dark-light pattern is structured. The difference between the two approaches is that light-and-shadow retains a third, secondary value statement within one of the two primary value statements.

Imagine that you are starting a painting. To keep the visual dialogue coherent, you divide the painting into a dark and light shape, one of which is more tied together than the other and so becomes the big shape for the painting. If you left the painting at this initial stage, you would have a dark-light pattern painting. However, if you chose to add a third value to either the light or dark statement, you would change the situation dramatically. By breaking down one of the value statements more than the other, you keep the painting varied in its statement—if the two shapes were broken down equally, they would both vie for equal attention. But by adding the third value into one of the two shapes, you bring even more emphasis to that primary shape, and this is where the "story" of the painting—in light or shadow—is commonly told.

The key to linking the third value to one of the two primary shapes lies in preserving a close value relationship between the third value and its host. For example, if you add your third value to the shadow shape, that value must be darker in value then any value occurring in the light shape—if the third value becomes too light within the shadow shape, it will appear to cut a hole in it. Correspondingly, if you add the third value to the light shape, then that value must be lighter in tone than any value in the shadow shape, or else you will cut holes in the light shape. The rule of thumb for attaching the third value in light or shadow is: the darkest light must be lighter then the lightest dark, and the lightest dark must be darker then the darkest light.

Local tone typically portrays a quality of light that exists when there is no direct light source. It is based on the breakdown of three value statements created by local tones within the subject. Light-and-shadow, conversely, is the product of a direct light source from which contrasting shadow and light shapes create the primary value statements, modified by a third value that is closely linked to either the light or dark statement. As you can see, these two visual approaches are defined by different qualities of light and reflect diverse visual properties.

Local tone, however, may occur in a light and shadow painting—this results from interpreting a situation that was once local tone and dividing it with a shadow shape. In effect, you are dividing a local tone painting into two whole statements, shaped by shadow and light. For example, a white house in a local tone painting appears as one whole value and color, but when direct sunlight falls on that same house its mass is divided into two separate values and colors. What remains after the division of groupings into light and shadow, is a sense of local tone in which values are linked within the darks and similarly in the lights. As you can see, light-and-shadow is a visual approach based in part on fundamentals borrowed from both dark-light pattern and local tone.

In addition to the three characteristic value statements, there is a set of rules that apply to the depiction of forms in a light-and-shadow painting, which define the sequential range of values characteristic of direct light falling on objects in a scene. Before we enumerate these rules, let me offer a word of caution: although they consist of observed properties of light creating shadows, try not to be too literal with them—they will only end up appearing labored or formulaic. Ideally, you want these principles to contribute creatively to the visual dialogue, rather than providing a statement of laws of physics. It is the visual dialogue that takes precedence, but the rules of light-and-shadow can help locate where to introduce the third value or detail that tells the painting's story, either in the light shape or in the shadow shape.

To illustrate the characteristic range of values within a light-and-shadow scene, imagine a white ball sitting on a white table, with a single direct light source illuminating the scene from above. Immediately, you notice that the scene is divided into two shapes: light and shadow. As you look closer, you begin to differentiate values within the two primary shapes. In the light half you observe the close groupings of the values in light and, in particular, a *highlight* that is the reflection of the light source. The highlight is lighter than the other values in the light grouping because it reflects the actual light source. As the light bends around the sphere, it meets the shadow shape where you see a soft edge called the *halftone*. The halftone is half in the light and half in the shadow, a fifty-fifty mixture of both light and shadow. It is actually a neutral soft edge that bridges the light and shadow, but sometimes a halftone can be a small detail shape that adds to the drawing of the two primary shapes. The true drawing in a light and shadow painting happens right here in the halftone where light and shadow meet.

Next we move into the shadow shape at the bottom of the ball, where all of the values are darker in relation to the light shape just described. Just under the half tone, there appears a dark band that wraps the sphere—the *core dark*—which is the true value of the sphere in shadow. Under the core dark, appears a lighter value called the *reflected light*, comprised of light bouncing from an adjacent or nearby surface, reflecting back into the shadow and brightening this area. The reflected light is still darker than the darkest light in the light shape, because it lies within and is, in a sense, the property of the dark shape. Under the reflected light, where the sphere touches the table, appears a very dark note that is small in size—the *accent*. The accent is the darkest value contained in the shadow and sits between the shadow-side of the sphere and the cast shadow. Finally, the *cast shadow* is the shadow of the sphere directed onto the table. It is lighter than the accent, but darker than the core dark.

In painting this scene, if you render these changes of value as the light moves across the ball onto the table, the result will depict a sphere in all its roundness, a form created of light and shadow featuring properties far more diverse in value than those applied to form in local tone. Joaquin Sorolla's painting, *Children on the Beach* (*Ninos en la playa*) is a work that contains all of the properties of light and shadow. In particular, the boy wearing a white hat captures the full range of values in light and shadow.

The following two lists enumerate I) the order of the value properties of light as it moves across an object and II) the value range of those properties in descending order from lightest to darkest. Though the properties of light and shadow should enable, not enslave, the visual dialogue; the physical characteristics are important to get right.

Properties of Light and Shadow

(The movement of light across an object)

1. Highlight

2. Light

3. Half tone

4. Core dark

5. Reflected light

6. Accent

7. Cast Shadow

Value Range of the Properites of Light and Shadow

(From lightest to darkest)

1. Highlight

2. Light

3. Half tone

4. Reflected light

5. Core dark

6. Cast shadow

7. Accent

GRADATION

Gradation is the procession of a visual element moving in one direction, thus endowing a shape or whole painting with a sense of movement. It makes more sense to use gradation with a light-and-shadow approach than it does with local tone, because gradation enhances the natural movement of light across a scene. As light moves across an object, its values grow darker and may gradate in color, too. In a light-and-shadow approach, gradation fits hand-in-glove with the properties of light, whereas in local tone there is no one direct source to create this movement, although gradation can occur within local tone too.

Many painters have used gradation within light and shadow. Rembrandt spent his entire life dealing with just this approach. His classically realistic style is famous for numerous abstract elements that heighten the visual dialogue. Richard Diebenkorn used gradation with local tone in some of his abstract works. Look at a variety of paintings by different artists using this approach, to see how the properties of light-and-shadow and local tone can be worked out in different ways.

FRONTAL LIGHTING

This visual approach interprets a light source placed directly in front of the subject, on a line between the artist and subject. The entire scene is bathed in light, with small slivers of shadow shape. Without these narrow shadow shapes, frontal lighting would be similar to local tone, in that you are interpreting a scene that depicts values within one light grouping. A frontal light painting should still retain its kinship to a light-and-shadow approach, wherein the light and shadow values work as separate shapes. Most of Lucian Freud's paintings use frontal lighting, suggesting a local tone look with slivers of clearly defined shadow shapes.

SILHOUETTE

Silhouette features a backlit lighting scheme, which is just opposite to that of frontal lighting. A backlit subject may be a figure standing in front of a window, or a tree in front of the sun, but it can also occur in conjunction with a local tone approach, wherein a dark shape is framed by a light shape. Since there is no movement of light properties, a local tone silhouette is typically flat like a dark piece of paper on a white background. In a light-and-shadow scene, the silhouette properties of light create a dramatic visual effect as the light shape carves out the silhouette. With the light bending into the shadow, the movement grows darker towards the center, until the core dark runs right down the middle of the silhouette. There may, or may not, be a cast shadow; but if there is one, it remains part of the dark silhouette shape, thus completing the logic of the visual statement. Many of Monet's haystacks use a silhouette approach.

COLOR

Color as a visual approach promotes the theme of one color throughout a painting, in a way that emphasizes that color's unique range and diversity. For example, you might take the color yellow as your theme and create a visual statement based on an arrangement of various yellows: yellowish browns, yellowish grays, and pure yellows. You might include lemon yellow, cad yellow medium and yellow ochre. With each different yellow, you define a new shape. The result is a painting that reads as yellow, with an orchestration of separate color statements lending depth and richness to the canvas.

Because of the diverse array of yellows, this approach differs from *color harmony*, which typically unifies a painting's surface with one kind of color. In order to make color work as a visual approach, you will need to build it on a foundational value structure. A light-and-shadow or local tone scheme might form the underlying framework for the color. When color dominates a painting's statement, the whole painting will speak first of yellow, before addressing the underlying visual structure, and it will do so not just in one yellow but through a whole symphony of yellows.

There are not many world famous paintings that embody this visual approach, although a number of talented contemporary artists are actively painting this way. Understanding the color as a visual approach requires a basic understanding of other approaches first, in order to supply the underlying value scheme to support it. With a better understanding of how paintings function visually, it will become an easier approach to understand.

3

THE HISTORICAL EVENT OF PAINTING 1450-PRESENT

The history of art traces the evolution of painting from its crude, early literal depiction of reality to its current interpretive statements of sophisticated visual intelligence. Though humans have been creating art for tens of thousands of years, most of that time artworks were not based on a visual dialogue. They served a separate, more practical, purpose. Most art history books trace the origins of art to the early Venus sculptures and cave paintings over ten thousand years old. These works were more about literally depicting subject matter than exploring the interplay of shape and color. The early purpose of painting was to convey a message that was about the surrounding literal reality, not about visual composition.

The historical growth of visual intelligence is like the development of any idea that we start with and bring to fruition. We start with a nascent, unformed concept that is plausible but not yet manifested. Similarly, an artistic idea starts out as a crude concept; but as we shape it into an idea, it becomes more complex, more sophisticated. The process of art is similar to that of baking bread. You begin with a simple ingredients: flour, water and yeast. As you mix the baking elements together, they form into dough, a mixture that we press, roll, and mold into a state in which the yeast can thrive. In its more complex state, the dough holds together for one purpose—to become a loaf of bread. When the dough is oven-ready, we slide it in and wait for the dough to finalize itself. When the loaf is done, the event of baking is over, and all of the previous smaller steps having been realized in its final state. Similarly, individual artistic works start out as simple concepts that progress into a more complex and sophisticated expression.

You might say that the history of painting follows a similar progression. It consists of one continuous dialogue carried on from artist to artist over centuries, culminating in our present understanding of the visual language. In order to understand how this language evolved, let's take a ten-minute tour of the great artists and some of their contributions to this ongoing dialogue.

In art history, the self-conscious evolution of visual language began in earnest about six hundred years ago, during the Renaissance. In the 15th century, two artists, in particular, changed the way painting made visual statements. They depicted subjects valued for their own visual integrity, instead of rendering them in the service of religious or political ideology. These painters were the first to complete paintings with a singular visual statement that by-passed social, cultural and religious hierarchies and brought autonomy to the canvas. In so doing, they opened the door to bringing visual principles to a painting for their own sake, instead of representing them as part of a broader commentary. For the first time, the artist's perception operated directly on the canvas, freed from the constraints of patronizing control. What separated the work of these two artists from what came before was their focus on the process of rendering a subject in purely visual terms—a focus on pure perception that freed the visual experience from its previous indenture to political or religious ideology. In supplanting social or religious dogma with a purely visual purpose, these two artists stood out as innovators. Prior to these two, painters had been consciously applying visual elements to their work, but these elements had not yet coalesced enough to free the work from external reference. In other words, they had all of the elements "to make the bread," but they lacked the heat of inspiration that "baked" these elements together into a final spontaneous, compelling and independent statement.

1450-1500

The two mystery artists who exerted such a profound effect on painting were Hieronymus Bosch and Pieter Bruegel the Elder. I consider them the first artists in the Western Tradition to attain such a level of visual and artistic autonomy in their work. It can be argued that their paintings were still picturesque and their content somewhat conditioned by the concerns of the church and society, but they both in their own ways broke loose from the literal mindset that had been directing artists for thousands of years. In finding ways to free themselves from prevailing hierarchies of thought, they still worked within their general guidelines, but began to explore the world in purely visual terms. Contributing to this new creative orientation, was the development of oil as a paint medium. It allowed the artist to work more freely. Unlike earlier materials—such as beeswax, fresco, or oils of unstable consistency, which made painting such a gruelingly slow process and inhibited the flexibility to explore artistically—the invention of a reliable oil medium sped up the painting process. Technological innovation aside, these two pivotal artists had the insight to create new visual approaches, characterized in Bosch's work by a consistent pattern of design, and in Breugel's by a more sophisticated use of tonal relationships.

1500-1600

The late-Renaissance produced a wide collaboration of great artists who pushed the visual dialogue into new territories. Titian, Rembrandt, El Greco, Rubens, Van Dyck, Velasquez, and Vermeer dominated the 16th century, taking visual understanding to significantly new heights. These painters took the properties of light and brought them onto canvas with a visual coherence and power never seen before. Each one gave dramatic new insights into the narration of light.

El Greco

El Greco was the only artist of this era who focused less on the language of light and more on the grammar of shape. He used some of the shadow properties that the others had explored, but subordinated those elements to the visual break-down of shapes. El Greco used light and shadow as a visual approach, but it was more to break up the painting into an array of unique shapes that were compelling for their own composition, rather than for their definition of light and shadow. He applied this unique distortion of shape to his subject matter and would often reinterpret the literal image to fit his created pattern of shapes. This "poetic license" shocked his patrons, but he kept at it even in the face of mounting pressure and disapproval. Four hundred years later, El Greco's work would have dramatic impact on two of the most important painters of the 20th century.

Rembrandt

Contemporary to El Greco, Rembrandt stands out for his profound understanding of light on a poetic level. Rembrandt captured the atmosphere of light and brought to canvas a vitality of paint quality and psychological depth that had never been seen before. He provided a level of expressive truth to his work that depicted more the event of light itself rather than a literal depiction of subject matter.

1700

The 18th century was a period of limited innovation. There were good painters working, but their accomplishments, relatively speaking, took a step backward from the Renaissance. The century produced many portraits of aristocrats in powdered wigs and numerous flowery landscapes, mostly conceived with a slavish attention to detail that was characteristic of first-level social imperative. Goya added excitement, Gainsborough contributed some accomplished landscapes, and Fragonard lent a painterly feel; but none of them accomplished anything that would expand the visual dialogue and affect later generations of painters.

Goya

Goya was perhaps the noblest painter working in the 1700's. Although his works opened no significant doors to visual truth, they did portray a strong sense of tonal value and expression, which most painters of the era had let go to seed. In Goya's use of value and color, I see an apparent thread of influence extending to Manet, who, in turn would later strongly influence Monet—one of the keystone painters in the modern revolution.

1880-1900

The evolution of visual intelligence remained in hibernation until the latter half of the 19th century, when Manet, at mid-century, and Monet, in the 1880's, provided a wake-up call. The great innovations of the Renaissance were still hanging in mansions and museums, but they needed to be dusted off. Perhaps the impetus was provided in part by the development of photography, which created a new infatuation with the language of light and freed painting from the obligations of literal rendition. Whatever the reason, 19th-century artists started to re-examine visual principles. Creativity came to life with a vengeance that pushed visual understanding to a whole new level. The impact of the resulting body of work carried over full-throttle into the 20th century, and remains a powerful influence to this day. The painters of the late-19th century took painting to a level that was based on visual truth rather than social conformity or religious dogma. In the 20th century, a new crop of painters would explore the visual world on their own terms, and their work would inspire successive generations of experimental artists, opening doors for later artists to explore even further the poetry of the visual world.

This pivotal era kicked off with the impressionist painters—Monet, Renoir, Pissarro, and Morisot—coming together and supplying new inventions, never seen before. Manet never jumped on the impressionist bandwagon. A transitional figure, his paintings retained an archaic, burnished look was more characteristic of the mid-1800's.

Monet

As ringleader for the impressionist movement, Monet took the existing visual language and expanded it to include even more color and atmosphere. Although the group around him caught onto the style that he captured in his work, none of them personalized it the way he did, by creating a unique bond of color and value.

Monet was unique for his ability to tell a story in visual terms. His use of the interactions between color, shape and value broke new ground in the way painters depicted the world around them. His radical new viewpoint challenged traditional visual conventions. Though Monet's abstract vision was often criticized in his own time as too wild and sloppy, today his work is fully accepted and considered almost classical in comparison to contemporary innovations.

There were many artists of the late 19th century who painted outside the group of impressionists. Sargent, Sorolla, Degas, Cassatt, Gauguin, Zorn, Van Gogh, and Cézanne each developed a unique and highly individualized style in their work. Monet's style was unique as well, but the cadre of impressionists who jumped on his bandwagon soon turned his personal style into an "-ism," even though they did not paint with his sense of visual purpose or clarity. In my opinion, there were only two artists who transcended the doctrine of impressionism: Monet in Europe, and Twachtman in America. Both shared a vision of light, color and atmosphere that was new and commanding.

Twachtman

Twachtman was an American painter, whose breakdown of spatial design was comparable to Monet's, yet inventive in its own way. He worked with simple value shapes, like Monet; however, his [subtle] orchestration of shape and color harmony provided a distinctive approach.

Sargent

Sargent exemplified the rare artist whose work effortlessly combined classical training and inspired intuition. Although his visual statements were far from radical, he reached a level of technical mastery and spontaneity that easily surpassed painters known for more innovative styles. I fully believe there comes a time in an artist's life where the artist needs to achieve a level of technical proficiency that frees the creative process to express itself as naturally as the visual world strikes the eye. Sargent embodied the uncanny ability to effortlessly balance formalism and spontaneous expression. He did not overstate the ideas that went into his work, nor did he espouse a particular movement. Instead, his paintings stand out for their blending of inspiration and formal clarity.

Van Gogh & Gauguin

Van Gogh and Gauguin were a pair of painters bonded by a spirit of innovation. In their search for new visual statements, they each tried to separate the visual essentials from the literal world; as a result, their work embodied a strong visual authority. Heroically, they brought a zeal for expression and exploration to painting, which paved the way for future artists to explore with less inhibition. Although they were rejected and scorned by the general public, today even the casual observer recognizes their works as masterpieces.

Van Gogh was more classically trained then most people realize. He fully understood painting's formal underpinnings and executed accomplished works of realism before cutting loose to paint the works we know him for today. Van Gogh may not have become a great painter, were it not for his ability, late in his career, to consistently reach the third level. He was the first artist known for his ability to tap the third level and paint with a pure gut instinct. A skillful artist for years before his stay in Arles, he arguably reached a rare level of creativity that transformed him from a good painter into one who could paint supernaturally. I doubt that he would have reached such an exalted level of creativity, had he conformed to accepted norms. Instead, he freed himself to paint with raw emotion and truth. He rendered a vision that pushed beyond literal barriers and brought his painting to a highly spiritual level of expression.

Cezanne

Often referred to as the father of abstraction, Cezanne is known for flattening down his subject matter into shifting planes of color and shape. His two-dimensional approach to the rendering of overlapping shapes profoundly influenced abstract painters of the 20th century.

The artistic creativity of the late-19th century evoked an individual perspective of visual reality. The artist became significantly identified by his or her approach, and this outlook would inspire artists of the next century to continue to define the visual dialogue in new ways. At the heart of these artists' new modes of perception, lay an intimate relationship with the visual reality before them. Painters were now closer than ever to resolving their works by purely visual criteria.

In the late-1800's, art progressed apace with the industrial revolution. Technological advancements raced forward at a rate never before seen, including inventions that would provide even greater freedom to artists. The invention of paint in a tube meant that artists no longer needed to mix the pigment and medium together. Portable easels allowed artists to paint on location with more spontaneity. The camera provided new sources to paint from and new interpretations of light. Politically, the old social hierarchies and entrenched monarchies were giving way to a new middle class with more money and power than ever before. All of these factors contributed to the formation of a new visual dialogue freed from the cant of religion and social repression. They enabled painters to innovate with a newfound authority. As painters discovered the play of shape relationships, they acquired a visual language that freed them from the strictures of literal rendering and encouraged a new creativity.

1900-45

In the 1900's a new generation of artists emerged from Europe, America, and Russia. In Europe there was Picasso, Vuillard, Bonnard, Soutine, Schiele, and Klimt. America produced O'Keeffe and Bellows. The Ukraine hosted Malevich, and in Russia there was Fechin, Malyavin, and Chagall. All of these artists started the 20th century with a shared desire to learn how life and painting worked as a purely visual statement. Their work gave birth to the abstract era.

Picasso

Picasso became a pivotal figure because of his ambitious push into abstraction and cubism. Yet his ultimate limitation as an artist stemmed from his becoming too wrapped up in dogma. He became more famous as a leading proponent of cubism, rather than for the quality of visual statements throughout his career. Picasso's early works spoke with power and integrity. In the first paintings of his cubist period, he made a dramatic leap into abstraction. These early abstract paintings were hatched out of visual ideas based on the relationship of shape and value. The sketches and paintings of the period predating 1910 were consistently honest and compelling. *Les Demoiselles d'Avignon*, painted in 1907, was his first attempt to break down the surface of a painting into an abstract composition, emphasizing shape. The work was built on a complex relationship of value and shape, and this dynamic still holds the painting together as a powerful statement. Picasso's talent was superb, and if he had kept himself from becoming distracted by the trappings of fame and money, he may have continued to venture into new territory beyond Cubism. But for Picasso, Cubism became more about the doctrine than it was about the visual search. His quest turned into an artificial approach to painting, focused on the rules of the "-ism" at the expense of visual creativity. The universal laws of painting apply to all styles and "-isms," but Picasso's later work lacked the same innovative drive. As his successive attempts became more and more about the "-ism," he abandoned his talent for visual innovation.

In spite of his shortcomings, Picasso's enthusiasm and talent for abstraction cannot be denied. He triggered the early stages of the abstract movement and popularized its expression, attuning new generations to its purely visual intent.

1945-70

The 40's through the 60's were marked by a collaboration of painters who strived to transform painting into a purely visual statement. Abstraction became the tool that enabled artists to interact directly with the visual dialogue—that interplay of shapes, values and colors taking place on the canvas. It had taken centuries for the artist to learn to see his subject in purely visual terms. [Abstract painters would make the final push toward making painting about nothing but the visual dialog.] With the arrival of abstraction in New York, a whole colony of artists flourished there, giving birth to this new phenomenon. They were led by Pollock, de Kooning, Motherwell, and Kline.

I mentioned earlier two modern artists who would be heavily influenced by El Greco—they are Jackson Pollack and Willem de Kooning, whose work demonstrates that, "new wine often comes in old bottles." The abstraction of shapes depicted in El Greco finds a new voice in Pollack and de Kooning. The resurgence of this impulse towards abstraction suggests that it may be an innate property of perception itself.

Pollack

Pollack's pervasive use of rhythm and pattern over the whole canvas gave his paintings an added dimension of depth. His use of equalization to orchestrate a symphony of shapes was reminiscent of Bosch as well.

De Kooning

No one pushed harder, or achieved a higher state of understanding in the New York group than William de Kooning. A native of Rotterdam, de Kooning was rigorously trained as an artist to draw true to life, realistically. In the 40's and 50's in New York, de Kooning made a conscious effort to depart from realism, in order to deal with what he felt to be a more honest approach to painting. In an interview he once explained that he had to abandon the literal imagery of realism, because it was holding him back from solving the problems in his paintings. In painting, the problems are always visual; and in bringing your painting to a state in which you can confront those problems directly, you are able to solve them. With this resolution in mind, de Kooning made haste in shifting his focus. Unlike Picasso, de Kooning remained engaged in the visual dialogue. Instead of becoming the champion to the cause of a particular "-ism," he pursued visual truth and clarity with a passion. Although the public labeled his work, "modernism," "nonobjective," and "action painting," de Kooning considered these labels important only to those who did not paint. He claimed to be only a painter, an individual. He believed his work was all about defining shape rather than acceding to the demands of a particular movement, and he held to this viewpoint in every interview. At the heart of de Kooning's visual statement was the interaction of shapes, which he rendered with constant invention and purity. His limitless imagination allowed him to create dazzling compositions for his whole life, without ever repeating himself. Nonetheless, he never lost touch with his classical roots in realism. His drawing skills remained the underpinning of his abstract work, and he used those skills extensively to create his unique shapes and other visual elements. Without his classical grounding, there is no way that his painting would have held up. His shapes continue to embody a richness that accords to the way shape is perceived in life. His singular interpretation of those shapes made him both classical and revolutionary.

Andrew Wyeth

At a time when abstraction was sweeping the art world, Andrew Wyeth retained a realist's look to his paintings while focusing intently on their abstract elements. He avoided the critical wars that attempted to supplant one "-ism" with another and worked alone in Brandywine, Pennsylvania, largely isolated from the New York art scene. Nonetheless, one can see an unmistakable similarity between how Wyeth applied himself to his watercolors and what the abstract painters were accomplishing in New York. He appropriated their shape quality and abstract design elements into his work, in a way that made his realistic subjects function on a purely visual basis. It's hard to know whether Wyeth appropriated this level of abstraction on a conscious or subconscious level, but his use of it evolved into a dramatic and innovative style. His interpretations of traditional rural subjects were endowed with a contemporary immediacy that continues to strongly influence contemporary painters.

Once abstraction ran its course as an artistic movement, artists began to flow in either of two directions—one leading into independent creative application, and the other leading into first-level confusion. For six hundred years artists had tried to expand the visual dialogue, by freeing it from ideological constraints. But now that abstraction had reached it purest state possible, many artists could not see where painting would go next. Into this vacuum rushed a plethora of schools and movements that dominated the art community and took creative initiative out of the hands of the artists. This led to an endless proliferation of "-isms" that are too many to list. What drives painting is the search for visual purpose, a passion for visual innovation that "movements" lack. You can argue that some of the new "-isms" do have a visual presence, but in the hands of critics, that passion of expression inevitably gives way to orthodoxy. To contribute meaningfully to the visual tradition, the artist—not the critic—must govern its visual principles. And the artist—not the critic—must keep the dynamic interplay of those principles as the main focus of the work. If visual clarity and drive are lacking in one's work, no "-ism" can hope to replenish it. The visual truth is always apparent on the surface of the work itself; it needs no justification or explication. By the 1970's, Modernism had become a cliché, and the art world was infected with the myth that you had to be part of some movement to be of interest. Just about everyone wanted to jump onto the bandwagon and tout a particular movement or style. Many artists painted to an "-ism," and museums are still full of their second-rate efforts lacking either creative authority or true artistic vision.

As I said before, most artists, students and collectors suffer from a lack of education in true visual principles. Artistic works may come out of places that do not have the teachers or resources to teach the visual dialogue, but those artists must rely solely on intuition. Clearly, one who has access to such teachings has a greater advantage. The Western tradition of painting started in a few countries in Europe with a handful of artists. As awareness grew, its principles expanded into more countries and continents. The artist living in a desert village in western China in the 1880's, likely would not have created a painting that works visually because she would not have been exposed to the information that would have enabled her to grow as an artist. She may have painted from an intuitive mindset, but she was still going to be limited by not knowing what the whole tradition of painting had accomplished. Today, an artist from some remote town stands a better chance of creating meaningful art, because the information is more widely available through a broader array of media than ever before. On the other hand, you can be in the heart of Tokyo or San Francisco, where the volume of the artistic conversation is deafening, and still receive the wrong teachings. Misconceptions perpetuate bad criticism and the pursuit of empty "-isms." To learn what is needed to read paintings visually, the individual must undergo a rigorous, classical regimen, taking years to train the eye to read visual relationships.

It is a matter of finding the right sort of teaching that determines a painter's integrity. No easy task, especially now. With so many movements and "-isms" shaping the art world, the evolution of painting—which has taken over six hundred years to develop—appears to have come to a standstill. Today's artist must fight through the literal-mindedness and the cant of "-isms." He has to move beyond social standards and fashions that will change on a dime, in order to find a visual integrity that can withstand the whims of taste. Artistic quality is determined by the visual composition of the work itself, which will remain intact no matter how society changes. These are the universal truths that underlie the aesthetic experience. "-Isms" come and go, but the visual dialogue is universally constant. As a student, you need a logical format for your artistic decisions to makes sense. An understanding of visual principles will give you the clarity that you need. In searching for artistic truth, you must look to the visual logic.

The latest "new thing" is called Shock Art. The idea is to provoke the viewer in the most degenerative way imaginable. As you might have guessed, it's not a tough accomplishment. Shock art is just another movement short on visual quality and long on titillation. Had these artists seen the paintings of Egon Schiele, they would have encountered work that shocked not just with its content, but even more for its astonishing blend of haunting shapes, lines and colors. They would have encountered work of unmistakable power and riveting beauty. Today's Shock Art screams for attention, but it only impresses those who cannot read paintings on a visual level. If only those who deem this work to be worthy could see through its literal and social pretense, they would see it for what it is: work of spineless visual quality, stripped of artistic truth—the Emperor's New Clothes.

Thankfully there were those who retained a close relationship to the truth of painting throughout the social commotion of the post-war decades. Painters like de Kooning and Wyeth worked all the way through this welter of "-isms" and stayed true to their aesthetic principles.

1970-90

The 1970's and 80's seemed to take a step away from pure abstraction. The era produced a new group of realistic artists, whose embrace of abstract principles contributed importantly to the unfolding history of painting. While de Kooning and Wyeth were still working and generating inspiration in these decades, the list of influential new artists emerging from their shadows included Richard Dieben-korn, Wayne Thiebaud, Lucian Freud, and Wolf Kahn.

Richard Diebenkorn

Although the abstractionists had brought their movement to its purest form in the 50's and 60's, painters like Diebenkorn found a way to give it new articulation. His best works are a blend of representation and abstraction. Diebenkorn's subjects often remain identifiable, but verge on a level of abstraction that appears ready to dissolve into pure visual dialogue. Always giving an innovative twist to the known, his sense of light and atmosphere brought new visual clarity to his California subjects.

1990-Today

From our contemporary vantage point, we have a full view of the evolution of painting and the freedom to utilize it as pure abstraction or as some blend of abstraction and realism. The point of painting is not to look for the next new thing, but to try to push the limit of what is there on an individual level. Exploration of the visual dialogue will never become passé, unless it lapses into pat, first-level formulation.

Our knowledge of the visual dialogue is much better understood than it was even 50 years ago. Its understanding will continue to grow, not as a taught subject in academic classrooms, but as the result of the creative process of painting. The visual dialogue belongs to the interaction of shapes on canvas—to the way they speak to one another and to the types of demands they impose on the imagination of the painter. The finished work, in turn, inspires a further discourse with other painters, and other generations of painters. In short, the visual dialogue is an organic and ongoing conversation of shapes, markings, signs and ciphers that draw on the collective unconscious and communicates the deepest secrets of the body and spirit.

4

THOUGHTS ON THE
PAINTER'S LIFE

Painting is not reproduction ...

Knowing how to use the visual elements and approaches makes a painter's life infinitely more manageable. As a set of organizing principles, the visual elements and approaches provide a logic that helps to shape the overwhelming influx of visual stimulation into a coherent visual artifact. They are the chords and scales that enable us to create melody and harmony with paint on canvas. Certainly, there are easier ways to translate empirical experience into an aesthetic statement. You could slavishly copy a photograph, reproducing every value and color note placed in front of you, but the result would be lifeless and dull. Understanding the elements and approaches frees you to *interpret* visual reality and to bring to life its human component. All art is based on the perception of human beings looking at trees, skies, plates, cups, rivers and figures. This ultimately is what draws us to good art: the identification with the emotion of the artist.

Order from chaos ...

A visual principle can be the visual statement that a whole painting speaks about, or it can be one of the visual elements that work within it. In the real world, we are constantly bombarded with random visual information. With our visual environment in constant flux, always reshaping its visual relationships, making paintings can feel like trying to hit a moving target. It can be difficult to decide how to apply those relationships in our work; but, if you organize your perception logically, you can simplify that vision so that the painting speaks to one moment of perception and captures its essence with compelling honesty. A painter's job is to capture a slice of reality and to make it eternal. That transformed bit of reality is really a blend of internal sensibility and external reality. That impact of the objective world on the artist's mind and senses is what ends up on canvas.

Think of a visual approach as a logical premise that brings a measure of reason and order to the perception we put on canvas. It transforms that perception into consciousness. And like a poem, a novel, an architectural design, a dance or play, each work is a finished piece of consciousness that the artist shares with her audience.

From the literal to the inspired ...

The visual elements and approaches provide a framework—a jumping-off point for a painting—not its conclusion. You could be looking at a scene that clearly fits a visual approach of light and shadow. If you paint it word-for-word, so to speak, just as it appears, you would be applying yourself to the expression of an obvious literal outcome. You can expect the painting to be dry as dust. However, if you were to consider the scene's interaction between shadow and light shapes, you might begin to see how they relate as whole shapes. If you then were to simplify one of the two shapes (ether the light or shadow) into a dominant mass, and break down the other so as to begin a cognitive dialogue between the two, you would be adding a dimension of awareness and insight that did not exist before in the literal rendering. You would be adjusting information to create a visual dialogue, and if the dialogue had enough interest and intention, it might grow into a visual story ... and you might be on your way to a successful painting.

But before you pat yourself on the back, you find that the scene is working with your light and shadow visual statement, but something is not quite right. Perhaps you need to adjust other elements within the painting. For example, you might be looking at a scene with many different colors that don't quite cohere. If you were to reinterpret those colors and reorganize them according to a more harmonic (or, perhaps, even more discordant) scheme, you will have made a conscious choice to enhance the visual statement in another particular way.

Whether you are merely observing life or creating a painting, get into the habit of being aware of the visual relationships that play out around you. How far those relationships can be pushed is part of the game. The art of painting is learning to transform literal perception into visual consciousness. You can reinterpret a scene by pushing its relationships until you are telling a visual story that is truly unique in its statement, and not just another knockoff molded from a literal formula.

Getting unstuck ...

As artists, we all struggle to open ourselves to new ideas and new ways of seeing. How many times have you found yourself standing in front of a canvas, boxed in by a problem, with no way to break through to a solution. Psychologists say that 90 percent of our thoughts are repetitious—we encounter the same memories, the same emotions and ideas over and over in various sequences. A different focus may bring a new outlook altogether.

For the artist, this is a good day-to-day practice, because when you open understanding, you expand the range of choices available to strengthen the visual outcome in your work. In the studio, the real time world confronts you with a flood of visual information. Reflexively, we reach for familiar solutions to bring order to the chaos on the canvas. But if you have the flexibility to abandon preconception, your potential for new visual discourse can be almost limitless. When you become stuck on a painting problem, embracing this mind shift can provide several ways to resolve it. This creative mindset is not only healthy for one's state of mind, but it puts you in control of your painting and returns confidence and commitment. Painting is a life-long treasure hunt for visual questions and answers, much like what drives a scientist to search our universe. It is a quest for universal truth, and in some ways the visual theorem is braided into that quest.

In searching for new answers with openness there is the possibility that you may move in and out of different styles in order to reach higher levels of painting. It may not be the style that makes the difference, but the approach that you interacted with that allowed the change to occur. You may make the shift in your work because the way that you were approaching the painting previously was becoming predictable and over-controlled. Control is needed in mastering your elements, but to become overly controlling may impede your learning, because it might make you too cautious in your work.

I once had the experience of losing the excitement and confidence I had displayed in my earlier paintings. My work had become contrived and lacked fresh insight. I was approaching my paintings with the same old ideas, and getting nowhere n my quest for new visual depth. This was a depressing spot to be in—I felt stagnant and knew that my works looked shallow. You might think that gaining complete control over the visual elements and approaches would have been satisfying enough, but in truth you never stop learning how to apply these principles. So I needed a new approach in order to move on. It was time to come to work with a new hat on. When you paint for a show and have deadlines, sometimes you can get stuck painting works that you are comfortable with—one, you know they will work out, and, two, you don't have time for trial and error. To resolve this I made a conscious decision to approach my next painting differently—to put myself back in the creative crucible by experimenting more. Doing so was both scary and rewarding. I was afraid that many of my collectors would not understand the shift that I had made and would stop buying my work. But I decided that I could no longer paint for them. I had to do paint for myself. The change was somewhat new, especially to those collectors who had just become aware of me, but I was actually moving back to how I used to paint when I was first coming to an understanding of the visual elements and approaches. When I was painting things that were not pushing my ability forward—the safe paintings—I realized that I was not going to learn from them. And that scared me more than disappointing a few collectors. By this time, I had been stuck for a couple of years, and when I awoke to what I was doing, the choice was obvious. I decided that my next painting would be different. It would be large, something around 50x50, and something that I could bite into. Its expanded size would allow me to become fully involved, and for a much longer time period than if it had been a small sketch. Before becoming stuck, my earlier works had been charged with an instinctive freshness that was liberating. They had opened me to new ideas. My new look had all of the freshness that I use to play with, and I was discovering new ideas again. My values, colors and shapes gained a greater richness. Although my understanding had intensified, my sales began to slow down. I didn't worry about it. My paintings remained toilsome to produce because they still sustained a high level of visual integrity and the shapes were just as hard to draw out, but I was responding to them more spontaneously. I chose to continue moving in this direction—to become myself again. It was risky, but satisfying.

Classical or Romantic Eye ...

Collectors have either a classical or romantic eye. A romantic collector will buy work for its subject matter and emotional appeal, whereas a classical collector will buy for visual clarity and technical accomplishment. Collectors go through the same sort of process that an artist does. Of course they proceed at a slower pace, because they are not actively working in the field, but their understanding is based on many of the same assumptions. When I decided to resume painting for myself instead of for my collectors, I had developed a recognizable style, my sales were just picking up, and I was beginning to make a figure of myself. All of these points argued against making drastic changes in my work, but I knew there were markets for all styles and that serious collectors would understand why I had made the change.

A smart collector with a classical eye can read all of the working mechanics of a painting. He will recognize how the painting was put together and understand the visual elements and approaches at work. He will buy a painting because it is structurally sound and appreciate it for its visual beauty, which is a quality separate from style, name, price, or subject matter. Because a collector with a classical eye will buy a painting because it is well-crafted, his collection is going to reflect a diverse array of styles and artists. For this collector, subject matter is secondary to the work's visual integrity.

On the other hand, a collector with a romantic eye will buy a painting based on emotionally driven, first-level reasons: subject, style, and name. It is perfectly justifiable to buy a painting because you like it, but if you are going to be a collector interested in works that retain their value, you may want to understand what works visually. There are many myths about what makes good painting, but few of them address a work's visual logic. Some refer to an artist's reputation, or particular style. Name and reputation are perhaps the worst criteria for judging a painting; there are many big-name painters, of all styles, who charge a killing for work that is completely lacking in visual integrity.

Style pertains to the superficial "look" of a painting, but if you buy into a certain style you are limiting yourself to a particular taste. Such collectors romanticize what painting is about and fail to develop a true visual understanding. This shortsightedness applies equally to painters whose work seeks to appease a certain stylistic niche. Where the collector with a romantic eye sees only the decorative outer shell, her classical counterpart has the ability to grasp a painting's entire structural makeup. The classical eye sees the truth and makes an honest evaluation.

Money ...

Some artists gauge their success by their popularity and prices. But success is not determined by what galleries you are in, or how much you make from sales. Money and fame breed a false sense of quality, because we have the notion that if a product is well-known and expensive its inherent quality must be excellent too. Think of the luxury car with a major design flaw that requires a massive recall. When a bad painting is sold for hundreds of thousands of dollars, there is no recall because most people are unaware of its flaws. I wish paintings would crash and burn when they fail, but they don't. A Van Gogh or Vermeer will sell for millions of dollars because they are brilliantly conceived works by two painters who played a pivotal role in art history. But neither painter had money or fame in mind when they painted these works; instead, they were driven by a need to articulate a visual dialogue.

Fear …

Fear is the ultimate killer of paintings. The moment it rolls in you begin to lose focus on what matters in your work. Fear usually rears its head in relation to a problem that needs solving on the canvas. The typical first response is to side-step the problem by postponing a solution. But side-stepping only prolongs the fear, and the thought that you might be in a better place to handle it later may never come to reality.

We allow ourselves to be driven by fear because we don't know the outcome—of a painting, a business venture, or a relationship. In painting, fear tells us that if we take the route of the unknown our painting will end up as a pile of muddy yuck, and that we will have wasted time and money. In fact, the opposite is often true. There is no magic paint brush that can resurrect a canvas and pull it from chaos to perfection. And even if perfection is achieved momentarily, there will always be another challenge to defy our knowledge and test our confidence.

As artists, we learn to embrace the unknown, and in that respect an artist's life is not too different from that experienced by the knights immortalized in medieval romances. Their search for the Holy Grail pursued an unattainable goal in which they never lost faith, in spite of confronting seemingly insurmountable obstacles and terrifying demons. The pursuit of great painting provides a similar goal with equally daunting ogres, but the good news is that paintings rarely draw blood. Dragons don't leap off the canvas, and if they do, they may be confronted with a healthy dose of perseverance and artistic integrity. The root fear in painting inevitably lies in what we don't understand.

What matters most in painting is visual quality, and if you make that your "Holy Grail," you have nothing to fear. A painting is good simply because it is held together by visual beauty. If you begin to worry about how you fit into the market or your reputation within some "-ism," your quest will be side-tracked. In staying focused on the visual statement, you can remove those anxieties and even tap the Third Level—the intuitive state of mind. Tapping the Third Level requires a mindset that frees you from judgment and brings you into the only reality that matters—the present moment. This is the only place where great art is made. You'll know you've arrived at that "Third Level" when you find yourself working through your fears and effortlessly sustaining your work's visual dialogue. In this "great, good place," everything that you need to happen in your work happens, and for a moment, at least, the whole universe speaks through a single painting.

Confidence ...

When you are confident and put forth the effort to commit an idea to canvas, you bring intention into your work. State that intention as clearly as possible and keep committing to it, until it rests firmly on the canvas. Commitment will convey a confidence to the viewer that says you intended each and every idea to be there just as it appears. When I critique a student's painting, my eye inevitably goes to those areas that lack commitment. If you make a 100 percent commitment to finish off every idea in a painting—big and small—your success rate will be high and your painting will have clarity and purpose. But if you're apprehensive and don't commit, that painting will never resolve itself. You may or may not be correct in your choice, but you will never truly know that until you put it down with full authority. Only once something is fully stated are you able to see it. If it remains undefined, then it is hard to see how it relates to the rest of the ideas in the painting. Be clear, be committed.

Effort ...

Effort is the ability to take your resources and concentrate them on a particular goal. In painting, your resources are your visual tools, and your goal is articulation of a visual theory. Say that you want to state something about color: first, you might select a color theory that would have the effect you envision for your painting, and then you would lay down appropriate shapes and values to provide those colors a stable platform to sit on. Next, you would make the effort to paint the color scheme, and with that effort would come a commitment to stick through the application of your idea until the whole idea is made manifest on the canvas. Your effort is always a measure of your commitment. You would need to put forth that effort until that commitment has met the goal of the painting. Does the painting say what you had envisioned? Has the idea become reality?

Commitment

Jim Valone was my first painting instructor. He was one of the few teachers who had something to offer in a fine arts department overrun by teachers who couldn't teach or didn't know what it meant to simply paint. I could trust Jim because he spoke with an uncanny wisdom grounded in a deep understanding of visual clarity. I glued myself to him and still remember the authority in his voice, as if his opinions and judgments belonged to a firsthand witness of all of art history.

One day I was having trouble with a painting. I couldn't commit to resolving some of the problems with the canvas, and Jim came around to take a look. I'll never forget his comment—I still use it in my own teaching. "If you go into the kitchen to bake an apple pie and it comes out as a cherry pie," Jim said, "something went wrong." Commitment is about carrying an idea through to completion. Generally, we have the confidence and make the effort, but perhaps we lack full commitment to the idea. We get sidetracked or turn the idea into another notion. If your intent was to bake an apple pie, then you should be pulling an apple pie from the oven. Sure, cherry pies are yummy, but if it wasn't your intention, it's just a happy accident—the next pie you bake may end up with something worse in it, like thumbtacks. You need commitment to complete a recipe.

A commitment to a visual statement can be as small as one shape on a canvas, or it can be as large as the whole painting. Often, a visual approach or other idea appears weak, because the artist didn't execute it with full commitment. There are generally two reasons for an artist's lacks of commitment. Either she thinks, "I'll finish the shape later," or "I don't know how to finish it off, so I'll just leave it as is." The first thought belongs to a painter who is either too lazy or too hasty to finish the statement. If you are too lazy, find a different calling or else learn to push through areas that you are indifferent about until you make them your favorite part of the painting. If you are too hasty and work so quickly that you jump from shape to shape like a pecking bird, then all that is needed is to slow down. Finish off each idea you start. For one thing, if you finish the shape or statement at hand, you won't have to come back later and remix that same value and color. You won't end up spending twice the time that you would have, had you finished it off all in one go when you had the value and color mixed on your palette. Slowing down does not mean that you have to paint at a snail's pace; it means slowing down your mental state. You can still paint quickly, but do so with a mindset that is calm, so that you resolve each shape. Think of it as putting together a puzzle. You want to have the patience of mind to fit the right pieces in the right places, rather then going so fast that you hammer in odd pieces in the wrong spots or completely leave out others. A puzzle always looks better if you put your full attention to completing it entirely, piece by piece (or shape by shape). A good painting feels like a completed puzzle, in which all of the shapes fit into their proper places and not one shape is left out. Missing even one shape can spoil a whole painting.

If you left a statement as it was because you just didn't know what to do with it, you're simply copping out. You still need to find a solution. A novelist doesn't leave a whole in his plot, just because he couldn't figure out what a character would have done in a given situation. As painters, we all reach our breaking point where we become limited by what we know. It is precisely this point, where we begin to struggle the most. A good painting will show you your limits and take you to your breaking point. When you find it, you also will have found your *learning point.* Put a hundred percent of your focus on the problem, because it will probably prove to be the reason you painted the painting in the first place. By working through painting problems, you directly weld yourself to your learning point. The answer can be found in many different ways, but the solution will inevitably be a visual one. Stick with it until you reach a solution, and commit to it as if it were the last canvas you would ever paint.

Originality ...

An original chef follows a familiar recipe but takes her own approach, which defines her unique style of cooking. She may have her own assortment of spices, a particular cooking time and temperature, even a selected way of combining ingredients. If you only follow the recipe in a cookbook, you might come up with a tasty dish, but there is little originality unless you put your own imprint on it. An original painter is like a chef with her own touch and style—she is simply providing a new interpretation to a common recipe. If you paint for yourself rather than for a collector, then you are already original. History and technique aside, you are still simply painting paintings. If you cut yourself off from your distinctive voice or personality, your paintings too will become dogmatic and lifeless.

Original Idea ...

We live in an age when most of the big discoveries about painting already have been unearthed. It is an exciting time to be a painter, because we have the benefit of all of this accumulated knowledge without having gone through centuries of turmoil to discover it. We have the freedom to expand on those ideas, but to do so we must first understand the foundation on which those concepts were laid.

There are conventional ways to apply visual elements and approaches to a painting, yet there will be those who have the vision to express new variations on the traditional standards and provide a new expression. They are not rewriting the laws, but giving more profound insight about them. If you look at the history of almost any invention, it has grown out of a basic understanding of a simple function and has evolved into a more efficient offshoot or expression. The early computer with its reels of magnetic tape and punch cards occupied a large room; today's laptop is exponentially more powerful yet fits in a briefcase. Painting is not a technological device like a computer or a car, the modern evolutions of which are technically superior. Instead, the evolution of painting represents an evolution of visual understanding that is represented and narrated on canvas. Painting is both visual and philosophical. The philosophy of painting is a system of conceptual ideas that relate to the visual experience of perception. As artists, we take those ideas and articulate them on canvas as a way of illustrating those principles in two dimensions. A new concept, or one that is based on a pre-existing principle, has to be in accord with the empirical integrity of those ideas. You cannot contradict those principles, but you can push their boundaries to gather a greater understanding of them, both intellectually and emotionally.

Painting and natural science …

As a painter you start by observing natural visual principles and expanding them through artistic statement into a philosophy of life. Paintings consist of a visual exchange of shapes on a two-dimensional field. Depth in painting (other then the thickness of the paint) is an illusion suggested by the interaction of shapes butting up to and overlapping one another. As a painter, you learn to see and think in two-dimensional terms, and the illusion of perspective and atmosphere is implied by blending an array of flat shapes to represent depth. Shape is defined by lines or edges forming a perimeter. Without these two visual elements—lines or edges—the space of the shape would keep expanding infinitely and never resolve into a statement. If there are no boundaries to contain a shape's inner composition—its value, color and texture—there is no way to form these elements into a shape. The *science* of painting—its visual makeup—is easily attained in the course of mere observation. The *art* of painting is about how you arrange its visual components to form a whole new statement that expands consciousness of the visual experience and enlarges perception. It creates an illusion that is greater than the sum of a painting's parts to give a transcendent experience of visual reality. To develop an understanding of the aesthetic principles that comprise one's art is an unavoidable precondition for becoming an artist. Once these principles are assimilated, they can be freely expressed and intuition once again given free rein in putting insight to canvas.

CONCLUSION

The purpose of this book is to shed light on what it takes to obtain higher levels of artistic achievement as a painter. Every painting we complete increases our awareness of the visual universe. Academic principles will steer us in the right direction, but it is up to each one of us to finish the journey by seeking new frontiers to challenge our unique, individual vision. Just as you can't explore America on Highway 66 alone, nor can you paint new imagery by slavishly following the precepts of old masters. Of course you will need to learn the skills and understanding it takes to put paint on canvas, but to tell a visual story in a unique way is to become a poet. Learn to take truth's melody and hum it in a way that is individually soulful to you. One who paints from the heart and retains the working mechanics of the visual elements and approaches is one who can paint spontaneously.

In the last few decades, astrophysicists have described the universe as a singular yet infinitely varied event that is expanding only to contract again into a state of singularity. This cosmic pattern is repeated in almost every form of life—the rhythm of breath itself. The life of the artist also conforms to this fundamental rhythm: expanding one's creative awareness and skills, only to contract them again into the space of a single canvas. In that rhythmic breath, we learn to free ourselves from the strictures of dogma, history and habit. We learn to loosen the visionary impulse from our imagination. In harmony at last with reality and illusion, we learn to inhabit the visual event. How far that creative experience will carry is up to you to discover.

THE END

www.ingramcontent.com/pod-product-compliance
Lightning Source LLC
Chambersburg PA
CBHW021007180526
45163CB00005B/1918